COMING OUT OF THE CLOSET

The Need for Women's Ministry in Such a Time as This

REVEREND SHIRLEY Y. COBB

Foreword by
Reverend Dr. John L. McCoy

Highly Favored Publishing™
BOWIE, MARYLAND

Published by Highly Favored Publishing™
Bowie, MD 20716 USA
highlyfavoredpublishing@gmail.com
www.highlyfavoredpublishing.com
Highly Favored Publishing™ is an entity of Highly Favored, L.L.C.

ISBN: 978-0-9835157-4-6

Printed in the United States of America

Library of Congress Control Number: 2011915738

To all of the women who
dare to come out of their closet of darkness,
take the hand of God and walk in the light of freedom . . .
and live!

CONTENTS

ACKNOWLEDGMENTS

Pastor McCoy

Someone gave me a gift once that had the inscription: "The angels on earth are the people with the magic of love for others in their hearts." This quote applies to many people whom I have had the pleasure of knowing, but I believe it especially describes one of the greatest men I have been blessed to meet, my co-laborer in the ministry and my friend, the Reverend Dr. John L. McCoy. It was because of the vision of Pastor McCoy that women's ministry came into existence at The Word of God Baptist Church and has spread abroad. It was because of pastor's vision that hundreds, soon to be thousands, of women like me finally know, and will come to know, who they are and whose they are and will know that it is okay to come out of their closets. Thank you, pastor, for your love, your leadership, your wise counsel, and most of all, for believing in me when I didn't believe in myself. I owe!

Mom & Dad

Without the two of you, I would not have been. No other child has been as blessed as I with such wonderful, loving, and giving parents. Thank you for supporting me in my work. Thank you for not giving up on me when others counted me out. I love you both very, very much! Mom, thank you for stepping out on faith and becoming a member of the first Virtuous Women's Ministry class at the age of 60! You were the first oldest member! Look how far God has brought you! Thank you again Mom and Dad for all you sacrificed so that your children could have!

Pete

My husband, thank you for making sacrifice after sacrifice in allowing me to carry out the work that God has assigned me to do, for the meals you missed and for the nights you slept alone as I traveled out of town. I thank God for helping us stick it out through some tough times. Thank you for putting up with me for 38 years! I love you.

Melanie, Stacey & Maurice

My children, God has blessed me richly by allowing me to give you life through Him. Life for all of you started as a struggle, from conception until your births. Nevertheless, God made death back up and behave. I have no doubt you will continue to put God first in your lives as you reach for your dreams. At my lowest point in life, when I wanted to give up, God wouldn't allow me to. Also, I knew I had to go on because I knew you needed me. You are the joys of my life! I love you very, very much!

Melanie, there were many who said you would not make it, but look at you now! I am extremely, extremely proud of the woman you are now and the woman you are still becoming. Your gentle heart has caused you to shed many tears. As I have admonished you, never allow anyone to change your ability to love, for God is love. Continue to stand on the wall, don't come down, and preach the unadulterated Gospel. I love you!

Stacey, I am extremely proud of you. The determination you have had, even as a child, has allowed you to achieve much. Continue to stand fast. The sacrifices you are making now will pay off after 'while. Continue to praise God through your dance, as the angels are forever around the throne of God praising Him day and night. Continue to wait for the Lord to give you who He wants you to have as He continues to prepare you to be ready to receive whom He sends to you. Truly, the Lord knows the plans He has for you, so "Wait on the Lord: be of good courage, and he shall strengthen thine heart: wait, I say, on the Lord" (Psalm 27:14). You are the epitome of the young, virtuous woman. I love you!

Maurice, my son, my little lamb. Your life started with such difficulties, but God, in His divine wisdom, ordained you to be. Your struggles to this point have been many, but God is allowing you to overcome them all through your karate, your writing, and most of all, through the beauty of music. Continue to remember that with God all things are possible. Think big, and never give up on your dreams. Believe in yourself. Look out world, and get ready for Moe! I love you, and I am extremely proud of you.

Hannah

I thank God for the day He brought you into my life to be my daughter. You are such an inspiration to me as you persevere daily through your many, many struggles. Thank you for all you have done for the ministry, especially overseeing the chapter in North Carolina. I love you.

Dwayne

Thank you for loving my daughter and helping her become all she can be. You are more than a son-in-law to me; you are my son. Continue to be prophet, priest, and king of your house, allowing Christ to be the center of all that you do. I love you. Thank you and Melanie for giving me my first grandchildren, my "Little D," my David, and the girls, Danielle and Daliyah. They are truly gifts from God and already irreplaceable joys in my life.

Little D

My joy, my "Swheedy Pie," my first grandchild. The Lord knew I would need you at this time in my life. You are one of the greatest blessings God has allowed me to live to see. Reach for the stars. I know God has a great calling on your life. One day, people will say unto you even more than they said unto Timothy as a young preacher, I knew your great-grandfather, your great-grandmother, your grandfathers, your grandmothers, your father, and your mother. Be steadfast, unmovable, always abounding in the work of the Lord, and your labor will not be in vain. The only person who can stop you from accomplishing your dreams is You! I love you dearly.

David

My "Pumpkin," God blessed me again with another grandson. I know your mom and dad will train you up in the way you should go. Do not depart far from it. "Trust in the Lord with all your heart, And lean not on your own understanding [even when times get dark]; In all your ways acknowledge Him, And He shall direct your paths (Proverbs 3:5-6 NKJV). There just may be a Titus who will one day be awakened in you. I love you dearly.

Danielle

My "Sunshine Girl," God has blessed me marvelously with you as my first granddaughter. On June 23, when God delivered you from His right hand as one of His ordained miracles, my life changed again forever. You are fearfully and wonderfully made, and marvelous is God's work. Never allow anyone to tell you otherwise. You are a little virtuous woman. I love you dearly.

Daliyah

My "Precious Girl," my cup runneth over. God poured me out a double blessing on June 23, with you as my youngest granddaughter. When God delivered you from His left hand 16 minutes after Danielle, I will never be able to express the joy that flooded my soul. When I consider not just the moon and the stars and all that His fingers have created, I count my grandchildren among His magnificent works! You are, as well, fearfully and wonderfully made, and never allow anyone to tell you otherwise. You are a little virtuous woman! I love you dearly!

Kevin, Kenny, and Xavier

My godsons. I thank God for blessing me with each of you. You are grown now with families of your own. Always remember that no matter what you desire to accomplish in this life, you must keep God in the center of everything. I love you!

Veronda

I thank God for the bond He has allowed us to form. I have seen you come out of your cocoon, and you are developing into a beautiful butterfly. Thanks for accepting me as your mom. "Stay focused." I love you.

My Brothers and Sisters

Helen, Maria, Joe Jr., Linda, Michael, Carolyn, Anthony, Sharon, and Robert—thank you all for your love, support, and encouragement. Helen, Maria, Carolyn, and Sharon, I personally want to thank each of you for participating in the ministry. Maria and Carolyn, I want to thank you for assisting with facilitating. Linda, one day God will bless us to bring it near you. I love you all.

My Nieces, Great-Nieces, Nephews, and Great-Nephews

Reach beyond the sky. If you continue to put God first in your lives, He will direct your paths. I love you.

Ann & Carrie

Thank you for always being there. I thank God for both of you holding me up during hard times. Your undying support and love of the ministry not only has helped me tremendously, but it also has helped the ministry become what it is today! I love you both. Thank you can never adequately express my heart-felt gratitude.

Paul & Robert

My "Gentlemen Extraordinaire," thank you for the many sacrifices you made for the ministry, allowing your wives to do what they did and using leave to drive us on our out-of-town missions. Your love and support will never be forgotten.

Fran Jones

The "Moses of Deaconesses," God has allowed you to make history in being instrumental in training deaconesses. Continue to share what God has given you to help them be the best they can be to their pastors, churches, families, and the women whom God has given them to teach and support. Thank you for your friendship, your support, and your encouragement through the years.

Theresa McCoy

"The Encourager," thank you for all you do behind the scenes. Thank you for your support and encouragement. Your labor of love to the teens and the young women, with a desire to prevent them from going through some of the hardships we went through, will never go unrewarded. I know how much better we all would have been growing up had we had a "T" McCoy in our lives. A personal thank you for your influence in the lives of my children.

Diane

Thank you for being my sister and my friend for these past 30 years. When I look at you, it is a constant reminder that God is still in the miracle-working business because of what He has done in your life. Thank you for your love and support. I love you. (To Kei and Sam, thank you for being a part of my family)

Uncle Ronnie

Pastor Bynum, when the Lord asks, "Whose life was changed as a result of your spreading the Gospel?" my name will be at the top of the list. You were responsible for my accepting Christ as my Savior, and for that, I am eternally grateful. Thank you.

Zing

Thank you for all we have shared over the years. I will always hold the memories dear in my heart. I am very proud of you. I love you.

Pastor Eugene Brown

Thank you for the years of preparation. You were my first pastor, and I thank you for helping shape my destiny in the gospel.

Laura

Pastor Bynum, you have been like a sister to me. Thank you for your love and support through the years. Your strength and faith in God have been an encouragement to me.

Melanie & Leslie

Words can never express the depth of my sincere gratitude to you for all of the many, many hours over these past 13 years that you sacrificed in helping this dream become a reality. We have laughed, cried, and grown together from its conception to now seeing the book in print. I am eternally indebted to the both of you for taking time away from your families. These 13 years have seen you, Melanie, married, being called to preach the gospel, and now mother of four children. Leslie, you are married and now mother of two children. Thank you sooo much! I owe! Stacey and Moe, thanks for the many days of babysitting while we worked. Dwayne and Corey, thank you for the sacrifices you both made by allowing your wives to help make this dream a reality!

Cherie'

To my "Strawberry Girl," I am blessed to have been asked to be your godmother and to have you in my life. Stay focused, and God will allow you to accomplish marvelous things. You are a little virtuous woman. Keep God first. I love you.

Dawn

Thank you for adopting me as "Ma." I am grateful to God for how

He is continuing to bless you. Be encouraged. God is still in the miracle-working business. I love you.

Deacons, Deaconesses, Ministerial Staff, Mothers, and the entire Family of The Word of God Baptist Church
Thank you for your unending support and encouragement.

William F. Hulley
In memoriam, thank you, deacon, for paving the way for ministry at TWOGBC with the completion of the first Mighty Men's Ministry class, in which my father, Deacon Joseph E. Young, Sr., and brother, Minister Anthony T. Young, were members.

Henry Berry
In memoriam, the greatest example of strength and courage in the face of suffering that I have ever witnessed.

Jessie B. Williams
In memoriam, to a great pastor who believed in and supported the ministry whole heartedly and was responsible for doors being opened for us in southern Maryland.

FOREWORD

As we look back over 6,000 years of biblical history, we can see the progressive death of women. The ghosts of Eden, highlighted by the betrayal of Adam, continue to haunt women, even into this 21st century. As we search the annals of biblical history, Adam's death is recorded in Genesis 5:3, but in the entire genealogical record of Genesis 5, we find no record of the death of Eve. In fact, we find no record of any woman's death that marked any great epoch in history. Why? Could it be that every woman died a little on that evening when God returned to the garden after sin entered into the world? If the Bible is to be utilized as an instrument to strengthen the family, then we cannot ignore the fact that one of the great responsibilities of the husband is to "cleave unto his wife" (Genesis 2:24). Implicit in the word "cleave" is the notion of *firmly holding on to*, *intimacy*, and *loyalty*.

The most common interpretation of God's commandment to Adam to "cleave unto his wife" is that Adam's primary responsibility was to be Eve's covering, protector, and provider. Prior to the "fall," we can find no evidence or record of God communicating directly to Eve. We can assume, therefore, that part of Adam's cleaving responsibility to Eve was to teach her of the dangers of the garden as well as the deity of God. If this is so, Eve had every right to expect Adam to cleave to her—to be her covering, protector, and provider—not only in intimacy, but also in times of crisis, if only for selfish reasons. Eve, after all, was Adam's answer to loneliness and human love.

But on the evening following the fall, as Adam and his wife were hiding in the foliage of the tropical paradise of Eden and draped in hastily sewn together fig leaves, the eyes of Adam's wife were indeed opened in many ways. They were not only opened to the "knowledge of good and evil," but they were also opened to the betrayal of her husband. As God descended into the garden and His voice called out to Adam, Eve had no idea that her husband, in an effort to save his own hide, would use her as his scapegoat. But as the exotic birds ceased their chirping, as the playful monkeys temporarily ended their bantering, as the hyenas called a halt to their laughter, and as the lioness pulled her cubs inwardly, and all eyes were fixed on Adam, self-preservation seemed his only concern. When Adam responded to God's inquiry by pointing his finger in his wife's direction, all of creation knew that from that moment on, human loyalty would never be a guarantee.

"The woman whom thou gavest to be with me" (Genesis 3:12) were the words she heard that would plunge her into 6,000 years of pain and alienation. "The woman" would become the generic excuse for all of the world's woes: the easy excuse for men not living up to their responsibility. Be it succeeding in a career or supporting his children, overtly or covertly, *the woman* would be the convenient cause of all of man's personal, social, and political failures.

Because of the woman's turning to give to her husband the forbidden fruit, the couple was expelled from their garden paradise. The world became Adam's domain and the woman's prison. The Bible gives no indication as to when Eve encountered another female, but we can reasonably estimate that Eve had no other woman with whom she could share her feelings and emotions. Her world seemed full of angry men who saw women as the conduits of the curse that fell upon mankind. The world of the woman became an unending nightmare where womanhood was the equivalent of shame, weakness, and subjugation. She was sentenced to live, or I should say *exist*, in a world where her mind was dismissed, her beauty determined by her body parts, and her value measured by her ability to produce male children—none of which she had any control over. It seemed that what made the female a woman, her gentleness, her sensitivity, and her ability to connect with a man on a level second only to God Himself, bore little value at all. She desperately desired the companionship of another woman who would need only nod in understanding of her plight. Oh, how one called "sister" could have made her prison bearable. Sadly, in the absence of such, Eve died long before she exhaled her final breath and was laid in an unmarked grave only God knows when or where. I am sure she died with only the hope that her seed would one day rise up to bruise the serpent's head and release her from the closet of blame, humiliation, and alienation.

Then, one starry night some 4,000 years later, a "sister" whose name was Mary bore a male child in a stable in a remote, Middle Eastern village called Bethlehem. This child would one day become the Christ who possessed the awesome power to understand the pain of women, as He would reach out to women in love instead of anger or lust. One would witness that love by the way He forgave a woman caught in the act of adultery. On another occasion, He met a woman at a well and released her from the stigma of five failed marriages and the bondage of six relationships gone sour. On yet another occasion, he took the hand of a young 12-year-old maiden and said, "Talitha cumi;

which is, being interpreted, Damsel, I say unto thee, arise. And straightway the damsel arose, and walked" (Mark 5:41-42). Who would have ever known that some 2,000 years later the same Christ that Matthew describes as having appeared on earth 42 generations after Abraham would gently whisper *"Talitha cumi"* to a 42-year-old woman by the name of Yvonne?

In speaking such words to Yvonne, our loving and liberating Savior set off a chain reaction that has launched a dynamic ministry that is inspiring women from coast to coast. Yvonne, through hearing these words, has discovered her true identity and now ministers to every woman who will dare to seek true freedom. I have no doubt the liberation of Yvonne will not be confined within coastal America because its power is needed globally and, therefore, will transcend the geographical boundaries posed by the Atlantic and Pacific. I can say with great certainty that the miraculous spiritual resurrection of this one woman, Yvonne, has the potential to produce such a shaking in America that it triggers a spiritual tsunami of possibilities that can sweep women in distant lands into a new birth of freedom.

Women, such a tidal wave of freedom will not be complete without you. Never again must you settle for the second-class, demeaning status of a "dead woman walking." Women of this 21st century, you have an advantage to which our mother Eve was not privy. Eve did not have a sister with whom she could bond or commune. Eve did not have a female companion who understood her pain and walked with her through the healing process. You, however, have a spiritual sisterhood through which you can receive the support you need to rise up and walk in your newfound freedom. As Yvonne's pastor, I have seen the difference that such a ministry makes in the lives of women in our church.

This book can be your first step toward the new, magnificent, wondrously made, and reborn You. You no longer have to settle for life in the zombie-like state that many women in churches around the world find themselves. There are Yvonnes who are being transformed every day and everywhere by application of the simple words "Talitha cumi." As you read this book, hear the tender words of our living God whispering ever so gently, "Choose life" (Deuteronomy 30:19). Close your eyes and experience His transcendent touch as He embraces your hand and leads you where peaceful waters flow. Slowly open your eyes and see the world in the glorious splendor as in the day our loving Creator kissed the world with His presence. Come out of the closet and choose life.

--Reverend Dr. John L. McCoy

PREFACE

In Maya Angelou's autobiography, *I Know Why the Caged Bird Sings*, she describes herself as a "caged bird."[1] Angelou was three years old when her parents divorced. Soon after, she and her older brother, affectionately called Bailey Jr., were dispatched by train from Long Beach, California to Stamps, Arkansas. With "To Whom It May Concern" stamped on their wrists, Angelou and her brother were sent to live with their paternal grandmother, whom they affectionately called Mamma. Angelou and her brother were raised with strict, no nonsense, piously religious rules from their grandmother. Because of Angelou's starched and restrictive upbringing, she sought to escape the grimness of times through her love for reading classical literature, especially poetry.

Angelou's life changed forever when her father returned in 1936 and took her brother and her to see their mother in the big city of St. Louis. Young Angelou and Bailey Jr. stayed in St. Louis with their mother and her male friend, Mr. Freeman. Mother, as they called her, drank and danced in gambling halls, kept company with different men, and encouraged her "babies" to enjoy music, food, and have a good time. Initially, Angelou believed she and Mr. Freeman had an affectionate father-daughter relationship. She longed for the paternal closeness of his touches, which she naively believed were innocent. However, during these times, Mr. Freeman engaged in various inappropriate sexual acts with Angelou, explaining to her that the two of them were only "playing." However, one day, Angelou's mother Vivian was not home. While innocently fetching some milk for Mr. Freeman, he grabbed young Angelou and brutally raped her. Afterwards, he threatened to kill Bailey Jr. if she told anyone what he had done. Because Mr. Freeman knew how much Angelou loved her brother, he knew she would never disclose his heinous and brutal robbery of her virginity.

After this vicious act, Angelou explains she was sick to her stomach and tried to hide the hideous act that had just taken place. However, Bailey Jr. knew Angelou's disposition had changed. He knew *something* was different about his sister. His sister Maya was fading away right before his eyes. Bailey Jr. and Mother found evidence of the crime, and Angelou was taken to the hospital. While at the hospital, Bailey Jr. got Angelou to confess what happened to her. To add to Angelou's emotional torture, she was forced to testify against her attacker and felt she had to lie. After the trial, her rapist disappeared. Eventually, it was discovered that he was murdered. Because of misplaced guilt due to Mr. Freeman's death, young Angelou, a tenderhearted eight-year-old, sentenced herself to a prolonged period of self-imposed muteness, with the exception of communication with Bailey. She stopped talking and silently crept into a private world of woundedness, formidable fear, and gut-wrenching guilt, and she became a caged bird. She became a trapped, frail creature who was not forbidden to open the door of the cage but who was so imprisoned by what had happened that she did not know how to unlock the door.

The story you are about to read is about another caged bird. She never realized how much of a caged bird she was until her cage, a closet, was opened, and she came face to face with trying to *live* for the first time in 42 years! Her situation is strikingly similar to Angelou's in many ways: the naiveté of the victim, the location of the act in the, normally, safe confines of the home environment, the perceived danger of disclosure, and the long-term impact of the multiple acts of sexual violation. The stories are also very much alike in their gruesome, horrifying truth: the same thief (the adversary) stole from both Angelou and this woman what was not his to take.

What happened to the woman in her closet caused her to become introverted and very withdrawn, almost invisible as a child. This young woman grew up and became like Eve, the first woman, the mother of all living. Because of Adam's betrayal after the fall, something in Eve died that day. Her happiness, her joy—the essence of who she was—and most of all, her trust in her husband died, and they were never revived.

This same woman became like Tamar, David's daughter, who was raped by her half-brother and became a recluse. This woman in her closet became like other countless, nameless women in the Bible—a "dead woman walking." Except this woman was walking on a private green mile to a private execution—hers!

Did your closet experience cause you to feel you were not worthy of God's salvation? Did what was done to you cause you to feel unworthy of God's grace? Did you feel what was done to you was, to some degree, your fault? Perhaps you have been ridden with guilt and shame for the past ten, twenty, thirty, forty, or even fifty years because you felt what you did was unforgivable. All of our closet experiences may have been different, but let me remind you that Jesus came to set the captives free!

As women, we have been pushed to the background, been told long enough what we can or cannot think, what we can or cannot say, or what we do or do not have the right to feel. It is time to break the strongholds that continue to hold us captive and make a change, and we can do it through ministry. We need to change not just for ourselves but also for our children and our children's children and for the survival of our families. Until we learn who we are, whose we are, and how to love ourselves, we cannot truly love anyone else, no matter how hard we try. We have to stop walking as dead women. I know life is less than perfect. We did not have a say in the hand that was dealt to us, but we can control how we play out that hand. Women, it is time to live! To live or not to live—it is our choice! You will see from the following story that it is possible to live and get there from where you are right now.

About thirteen years ago, I met Yvonne in a ministry class. She was 41 years old when she entered the ministry class, a place where her life would change forever. Her story touched me because as a woman, I could identify with her pain and her hurt. We had many one-on-one counseling sessions where we shared and prayed, cried and shared, and prayed and cried some more. I asked Yvonne for permission to share her story, which changed my life, because I knew her story would change the lives of other women, as well. Yvonne struggled for years trying to become free from what happened to her in that closet, and this book is about that decision to become free.

This book was written to end the grueling nightmare of all the women in the world who secretly share closet experiences. It is designed to proclaim to each one of you, "You are not alone, and freedom is possible." Nevertheless, freedom is a decision—a decision only you can make. Will you forever remain in the grips of your past captors? Will you continue to struggle under the awesome weight of abuse and second-class citizenship in the kingdom of God? You must decide! Coming out of the closet is one's birthright. It is a right that *must* be determined. If you are sick and tired of being sick and tired of the pain, tired of the guilt, tired of the shame, tired of not loving yourself, tired of suffering from low or no self-esteem, and tired of dragging around excess baggage from one year into another, then there is only one solution. Extend your hurting hand to the healing hand of Christ who is waiting to bring you *out of the closet*.

--Shirley Cobb

1

YVONNE'S STORY

I was a middle-aged woman when I came to the place where my life would change forever. I had been married all of my adult life. I had also been in the church all of my adult life, having committed my life to Christ shortly after finishing college. For as long as I could remember, I possessed a desire to nurture people who were hurting. However, as a woman of 46, I was hurting. I discovered that my private pain had its genesis in a dark closet some 42 years earlier. I remembered the evil that happened in that closet as if it had occurred yesterday, for indeed, what took place in that closet has been revisited every day in my mind.

For 42 years, I had been haunted by the hands, hands that lured me with candy into the dark and hellish abyss of that inner-city apartment closet. I was imprisoned by hands that moved up and down my little body and in and out of my body cavities, hands that stole and snatched my childhood innocence. Every day that I lived, I remembered, and in one way or another, I wept agonizing tears because of those hands. I have never forgotten the cold and sinister hands that prematurely robbed me of the natural adolescent discovery of my sexuality and strangled my natural development. It seems that every major event in my life has occurred prematurely.

I recall the story my mom tells about the circumstances surrounding my birth. I was scheduled by medical estimation to be a late winter gift to my parents. My birth, however, took place seven weeks early. In retrospect, I see how demonic forces had attempted to destroy my life even before I was born. Oddly enough, those same hands that reached out in the darkness of that closet were indirectly and partly responsible for my premature birth. As my mother was rushing to the aid of the person who would later become my closet captor, she fell down the stairs and went into early labor. Ironically, my mother's helping hands were reaching out to aid the same person whose hurtful hands would later force me into a physical and mental claustrophobic closet of pain and torment. Those same hands would continue to rob me of the innocence of my childhood, the self-discovery of my teen years, the fulfillment of my marriage, the joys of motherhood, and even the abundant life promised in Christ until my date with destiny some 42 years later.

My mother's body was racked with pain all morning and early afternoon on the day she fell. When she could bear the pain no longer, she made her way with my dad on that cold, blistery, bone-chilling Tuesday in mid fall to the local hospital where I was born about 5:40 p.m. The year I was born was ranked as the third snowiest winter in history with 88.9 inches of snow recorded.

At birth, I weighed 5 lbs., 4 oz. The doctor remarked that my weight was excellent for a preemie born seven weeks early. According to calculations, if I had been born on my projected due date, which was December 25, I would have weighed close to 9 lbs. (because of babies tripling their weight during the last trimester). Because of my losing weight after I was born, down to 4lbs., 6oz., I was not allowed to go home with my mother. Back then, if babies were less than 5lbs., they could not go home until they gained weight. Now, because of advancements in medicine, babies are going home much smaller, and I probably would not have been kept in the hospital at all since my lungs were fully developed.

I often have wondered if my premature birth is where my bout with loneliness began. Could it be possible that a little underweight baby lying face up in an incubator in an intensive care nursery could sense the loneliness of the years to come? The incubator may have shut out the germs, but it also shut me out from the initial closeness of the person from whom I had come. No transparent crib could substitute for the need of human touch. Lying face up in a glass house denied me the right of being able to nestle my head in the warmth and comfort of my mother's bosom. Lying in an incubator denied me being cradled my first seconds, minutes, hours, and days after birth in the arms of the one who carried me. The steady beat of the buzzers and alarms could not substitute for the lack of hearing the familiar beat of my mother's heart. Being born prematurely forced me to be left in the sterile, but isolating, environment of a hospital, instead of in a crib next to the bed of my mother. The thief stole this from me even before he met me!

Ironically, my mother's helping hands were reaching out to aid the same person whose hurtful hands would later force me into a physical and mental claustrophobic closet of pain and torment.

Is it possible that one so little and so fragile could, from birth, be sentenced to live a life of loneliness? Is it within the boundaries of human providence that loneliness can be bequeathed by events that occurred long before one is born? I often have wondered exactly when or where loneliness became both my comfort and my curse.

Today, there is no doubt exactly when and where my pain began. It began in that damnable dark closet four years after my premature birth, but for 42 years, I held the secret of that closet and the identity of those hands. For 42 years, I had not so much as whispered the name of the misguided owner of the hands that violated me. For 42 painful years, I endured the unfair judgment of those who sought to interpret my quiet and withdrawn demeanor without seeking to discover the source of my involuntary exile from the rest of the world.

However, at the age of 46, as a married woman of more than two decades, I sensed I could not keep my secret locked within my victimized bosom or stowed away behind the mask of seething anger much longer. It was time to be free, and I desperately needed freedom. I panted for freedom as a thirsty deer pants after the waters of a brook.

Since my entry into the world of church, I searched for the freedom my soul longed for in religion. I became part of a small, charismatic church and got caught up in the almost primitive search for freedom from my pain. In this environment, my soul literally shouted to be free. However, I had failed to find any real freedom in the exterior expressions of charismatic praise and worship.

After being involved in this particular church for 18 years, I felt beckoned by a power much greater than I had ever experienced. A voice echoed from within the enclosed chambers of my unfulfilled bosom, *"Leave the land of thy re-birth Yvonne, and go to a land that I will show you."* So I left the familiar confines of my first spiritual awakening and, for a while, wandered in the wilderness of no church home. I searched here and there, always led by that unseen power to venture on to the next place. Then, one Sunday, I came upon what seemed to be the place to which the hands of God were leading. At last, I found a home, but I had not yet found freedom. The hands of the closet demon still clutched me tightly and held me hostage, refusing to surrender my struggling spirit. The haunting of those closet days daily emerged to rob me of the joy I felt rightly belonged to me as a child of God.

I became involved with ministry, and almost immediately, the Lord revealed to me my mission in life, my purpose for being born. My mission was to help other women become free, to become all they could be in Christ. I became so focused on helping hurting women that I, once again, pushed my need for freedom to the bottom of the list. I needed to be free of my closet captor, but in order to become free, I had to face him squarely and demand my freedom. In order to face him, however, I had to first identify him, and to identify him would be to open Pandora's box.[1] After all, there were so many other people to consider. Here was an already fragile and frail family that, in my estimation, probably could not withstand another crisis. It seemed that all my life I struggled with a fear of creating more stress on my already over-stressed parents. How could I even tell my husband now—after all these years? I had always dealt with my pain silently, privately. How could I, at this stage of my life, become an "issue"? How could I allow my cancerous pain to eat away slowly my chances for freedom? So, I agonized.

As I worked in ministry for the next four years, with every day that passed, my pain crept ever so slowly to the surface. My pain affected the way I saw the world and the way I responded to my peers, but mostly how I saw myself. I never attempted to enhance my outward appearance. I was always afraid that doing so would attract attention. I was talented, but afraid to show it. I had a mountain of love bound within my lonely heart, but could not fully release it. The shadow of the one in the closet loomed over me like an ominous cloud. I was the classic victim: afraid and guilt ridden, and I found safety in being silent and invisible. So, I waited; for what, I did not know—but I waited.

Then, one evening as a women's ministry class was being conducted, my closet captor appeared.

2

THE CLOSET

"He revealeth the deep and secret things: he knoweth what is in the darkness, and the light dwelleth with him." Daniel 2:22

One fall evening in 1997, as the women in the ministry class shared their horror stories, my closet captor manifested himself. I could feel his eerie presence. Amidst the maze of the tales of rape, abuse, and feelings of degradation, I could feel the cold hands of my captor once again. With memories as real as the pain of the women in that room, he taunted me with the 42-year nightmare of his devilish deeds. At that moment, I realized that as long as he was allowed such control over my life, I would remain in that closet forever. I knew that as long as he was allowed the safe haven of that dark closet, I, and millions of women like me, would belong to him. I was not willing to concede a lifetime to his dominance. When the reality of that possibility hit me, I decided to push open the door and not just come out of the closet, but run toward the light—the beckoning, brilliant light of freedom!

That evening, as I headed home from the ministry meeting, I was still reeling from the emotional trauma of having my closet captor return. As I drove down the parkway toward home, my vision was somewhat blurred. My mind was still wandering through the maze of haunted memories of the hands that robbed me of my childhood innocence and purity. The dreaded ghosts of

1955-56 seemed to race mercilessly through the dark corridors of 42 years like a horde of ravenous, crazed wolves, and I once again became that scared little girl of 4 years old. I arrived home as if through a sleepwalk. My husband was in our bedroom. My children were asleep. I was relieved that I did not have to carry on the usual talk about the affairs of the day. I do not think I would have made it through the conversation. I knew that someone would just look at my face and know that something was wrong. God was merciful to me.

As I saw the light from under my bedroom door, I thought to myself, *I dare not go in right now, for my husband will quickly see the guilt of my past and smell the stench of* (what I perceived as) *my sin.* I had never so much as uttered a word of such events to him or to anyone else in the more than four decades of my hellish exile in the land of pain and shame.

In desperation, I reached for the telephone and nervously placed a call to my pastor. I recall sitting on the floor of the hallway trying to collect my thoughts and trying to slow down my racing heart, almost feeling panic-stricken as I tried to maintain my composure. I felt as though I was physically in the closet again in the clutches of evil. The thoughts of my closet experiences seemed to be rushing from within my sour stomach as vomit seeking an escape.

As I dialed my pastor's number, the three rings before he answered seemed like an eternity. After my initial greeting, I paused. Sensing some trepidation, he inquired as to what was on my mind. I continued to hesitate as he continued to hang on, as if he could clearly hear my silent agony. *Dare I let these demons go free? Dare I share what I have so efficiently kept under the lock and key of silence and denial for these many years? Dare I open the door to my closet, to a man, no less?* A thousand questions raced through my mind. I shared with him the subject of our ministry discussion in an attempt to camouflage the fact that this subject was remotely reflective of any personal experience. As my voice reduced to a whisper, he seemed to sense I was speaking as a participant and not an objective observer. I felt comfortable speaking in a general sense of what the "other women" had experienced, not revealing any names or details because of confidentiality. I remember whispering. I remember feeling like I was fading away. I felt like the closet was muffling my sounds again. I could hear over and over again the voice of my closet captor, "This is our secret. You must never tell."

Several times, my pastor asked me to speak a little louder, as if in stunned disbelief. In reality, however, I could barely speak above a whisper, for the secret I was disclosing seemed much too horribly shameful to utter with any volume. Suddenly, but with a great sense of compassion, he asked, "Yvonne, are you dealing with something that happened to the *other* women only, or are you speaking of yourself, as well?" My hesitation said it all.

There was a long silence—a silence that caused me to be very uncomfortable. I began to weep. For the next few moments, I wept tears that had been welled up in my heart for over 42 years, tears that had been hidden from my mother, my father, my sisters, my brothers, my husband, my children, my church, the ministry, and the public. I wept the tears of a little girl who had done something very wrong, evil, and nasty, tears of humiliating shame. As I wept, I wondered what my pastor was thinking of me. I felt incredibly childish and immature. I attempted to collect myself, but I could not get a grip of any sense of solace. In that moment, it became clear why I had never disclosed my closet experience to any other human being; I did not want to endure the silence and, worst yet, the pity that such silence suggested.

Softly, as if searching for the "correct" response, my pastor asked if I was all right. I told him, "No, but I will be." I believe my reply was a vain attempt to regain the composure that seemed always to yield me less vulnerable and place me on some invisible level of dignity. It was getting late. I asked if we could talk again tomorrow. He seemed very reluctant to let me escape; nevertheless, we said goodnight. That night, however, was far from "good" or "over" insofar as I was concerned.

I do not believe I slept an hour as I lay there staring into the nocturnal abyss of the gloomy darkness. I searched for an elusive rest, only to find a fear of an unsolicited visit from the nightmares that marked my early years. I had no idea of knowing whether sleep would be a welcomed friend or a frightening fiend. I became envious of my husband who lay next to me so restful and unaware of my self-imposed wrestling match. Those hands had taken hold of me again, having reached across 42 years. Again, those hands seemed to strip-search me, groping over my private parts in an endless quest for some fiendish and demented form of diabolical gratification. Yes, it was *those* hands, which seemed always accompanied by the sound of heavy, beastly breathing resounding against the backdrop of the closet walls. At one point during that night, I could not tell if it was 1998 or 1955 again. I wanted to scream with all that was within me, but I repeated my actions of 1955 and said nothing. I have always felt guilty for saying nothing. After a while, I could see the faint images around my bedroom that signaled the fact that dawn was approaching. I welcomed the dawn. Oh, how I welcomed the dawn.

During the next several days, I unmercifully unloaded the weight of the closet years on my pastor, feeling somehow secure because of the vow of confidentiality for which clergy are known. I shared with him how one of my teenaged relatives would lure me into the closet while my mother ran errands. It began as a kind of hide-and-seek game that I was naively unaware I was playing. He would go into the bedroom closet and wait. As I played near the closet, I would hear a voice calling from within. As I edged closer, I could see candy in the hand of the closet inhibitor. As I reached out for the sugary treat, his hands took mine and pulled me in. As he sat on the closet floor with his knees bent and his pants unfastened, he turned me from front to back and back to front, trying to find the best angle to do what he was trying to do. He chided that this was our "little secret," and therefore,

> In that moment, it became clear why I had never disclosed my closet experience to any other human being; I did not want to endure the silence and, worst yet, the pity that such silence suggested.

I must not tell a soul. As his activities seemed to reach a crescendo of respiration upon penetration, I sucked on that piece of candy. I was confused. I have always felt ashamed to say that I did not know that what was occurring was inappropriate, perverted, abusive, and just simply wrong! After a while, I was released and nothing was ever said.

One day, I overheard a relative telling my mother what this teenaged relative had done to her. My mother's reaction said it all.

What was occurring on a regular basis in that closet was wrong, very wrong. My mother became furious, almost hysterical. She immediately summoned and interrogated me as to whether he had "done something" to me, too. In petrifying fear—hearing the screams of my mother and seeing the tears streaming down and that look on her face that I shall never forget when asked if I was hurt—I adamantly denied it. Promptly, my mother confronted the closet captor. He angrily denied he had ever touched any of us in an inappropriate manner. My female relative persisted that her charges were true. She was taken to the hospital to be examined by a doctor where it was confirmed the allegations were, indeed, true.

For years, I have regretted my silence. My trying to deal with the pain and trauma in silence caused me to become very, very withdrawn. My brothers and sisters often misinterpreted my silence. I was thought to be "aloof" and often classified as "weird." All the while, I struggled with what happened and my denial of it. To protect my sanity, every night in my dreams, I became the invisible child.

Complete the workbook lesson on "The Closet."

3

THE INVISIBLE CHILD

"For in the time of trouble he shall hide me in his pavilion:
in the secret of his tabernacle shall he hide me;
he shall set me up upon a rock."   Psalm 27:5

Throughout the years of my post-closet existence, and I say existence rather than childhood out of a now clearer understanding of the term, I felt invisible. I was looked upon, but never clearly seen. My body was "present and accounted for," but my person was AWOL. I do not speak of my invisibility plaintively but, rather, affectionately because in my invisibility, I found safety. If I could not be seen, I could not attract the hands.

Invisibility came with its share of costly prerequisites, and the first prerequisite of invisibility was inaudibility—silence. If one desired the safety of not being seen, then one must be willing not to be heard. It was during this need for safety that I developed the attribute, or liability, that would mark the rest of my life. To some, silence was a virtue; to others, it was an indicator that I suffered from some form of mental retardation or that I was highly intelligent, deceptive, and could not be trusted. To this frightened little girl, silence was merely a necessity of invisibility and survival.

Invisibility required silence, and silence required suppression, another costly prerequisite. That suppression was a total surrendering of my right to be heard or to confront my adversary.

I know now what I did not know as a little girl or young woman: such a trade-off only built a prison that held me captive, captive to the desires and wishes of others who were all too willing to have their way with little or no regard for my wants or needs. Such would come back to haunt me later in life.

The third aspect of my invisibility grew out of a friendship that began in the sixth grade with a neighbor, and later classmate, by the name of Robin.[1] Robin lived just around the corner from where I lived, and during the summer of '62, we quickly became friends. We walked to and from school together. We seemed to connect, as she also possessed a sadness of spirit that somehow seemed identical to my own. Her father was a pastor, and I enjoyed attending church service with her. I was allowed to sing in the choir, even though I never officially joined her church. It seemed strange that I felt more comfortable singing than talking, but there was an element in singing that freed my spirit to fly. My song was all I had. As a caged bird who could not escape the physical bars that imprisoned me, singing became my emotional and, greater still, my spiritual means of rising above that which bound me. This third aspect was extremely important to me as it provided a tremendous avenue of release and, therefore, promoted freedom.

There were times, after I began attending Robin's father's church, when I would dream of being pursued by hideous monsters and grotesque, satanic creatures. Perhaps such dreams were a result of her father's sermons where hellish creatures found in the biblical books of Ezekiel and Revelation would come out of the ground, or from the sky, and pursue the wicked. Maybe the origin of such creatures grew out of my closet experience. Night after night, as the monsters got close to me and I became tired while running, I would become invisible so they could not find me. I would watch and wait until the demonic beasts would imprison the others. The beasts would always take their victims through the floors to the pits of hell and torture them. The moment the monsters left the people, I would become visible, comfort them with my words, and assure them of my purpose to rescue them. I would then untie them, and we would join hands and form a chain. Then, I would stretch out my arm and fly the people to safety. Yes, I had the ability to fly! Flying was the fourth and most protective aspect of my invisibility.

The ability to fly in my dreams did not only occur in times of distress. Occasionally, before a chase, I would spread my wings and soar heavenward just to experience the magnificence of God's creation. I would fly high and peruse the majestic mountains, the beautiful countryside, the golden fields, and the green meadows of His glorious earth. The greatest feeling of such an experience was the eternal peace of being out of my tormentors' reach. Nothing else in my entire life has come close to the experience of flying. Night after night, I flew high above fear, anxiety, and most of all, *those hands*. Flying, I believe, was God's way, even then, of opening my cage and allowing me to soar as high as the eagle and to experience the physical, emotional, and spiritual freedom that was mine to possess. I believe it was God's way of letting me know, even then, that no closet captor could hold me because He had a work for me to do.

Only in my dreams did the door to this caged bird allow access to the heavens. But then, I would awaken, and the cage door would slam shut. *BAM!*

The one creative result of being invisible was that I would spend a great deal of time alone. In my solitude, I developed a love for writing. There seemed to be solace, serenity, and a sense of purpose in the written word that was not available to me in the spoken word. Even at 10 years old, romantic stories were my forte, and I spent hours writing idyllic, romantic tales of far-away places and characters who were very real in my mind. As the writer, I possessed the ability to create "happy endings" in their affairs of the heart. What delight I felt, with just a few strokes of my pen, to give those imaginary characters (mostly women) what was so elusive in my own hurting heart—a sense of real love and safety from villainous, familiar strangers. All too soon, however, their stories would end, and the nightmare of my own existence would commence again. Therefore, my best bet for safety was to be the "invisible child."

Even in the midst of my silence, I never doubted that my parents loved me. Perhaps the most stabilizing influence in my years of invisibility was the love of my parents. They demonstrated their love daily. My mother would deny herself the luxuries of a new pair of shoes or updated clothing for the sake of her children. My father worked multiple jobs, five days a week, and sometimes on Saturday, to provide for his family. When Daddy was home on Saturday evenings, my two older sisters and I would get great enjoyment from sitting with him for hours as western heroes like Gene Audrey, Hopalong Cassidy, or Roy Rogers rode across the screen. Then, late at night, my sisters and I were allowed to stay up with Daddy as he watched scary movies. We knew all about how Lon Chaney became the Wolf Man and Beli Logosi became Count Dracula. We were not frightened, though, because Daddy was there to protect us.

It was so comforting to spend this time with Daddy, although he often fell asleep during most of the programs. As I look back on those invisible days, I know now that the presence of Momma and Daddy allowed me to endure the pain and the anguish. Then, as now, I may have been invisible to many, but to Momma and Daddy, I was not invisible at all. I was not "slow." I was not a deceitful or defiant child. I was their special little Yvonne. I thank God for my parents every day of my life. Without them, I could not have endured the long night of my pain. In retrospect, I know their love for a child who chose to be invisible was the most visible element of my entire ordeal. Not only did my parents' love help me maintain my sanity, but so did my friendship with Robin.

Robin did not graduate sixth grade with me that year. That summer, she left to go live with her mom somewhere beyond Norfolk, VA. I truly missed her, for it was after she left that I retreated further into my cage. I no longer attended church. I was a caged bird again, but this time, I had no song. I went to see her several times, taking that five-hour bus trip, but it was worth it, being able to spend time with her again. We stayed in touch via phone, but as time moved on, the calls became fewer and fewer. We never talked about our years before sixth grade, perhaps due to tremendous pain we both experienced during our earlier years. I kept silent about the evil hands of my perpetrator, even to my best friend.

In my post-Robin years, even more than before, I was that child in my house who rarely said much. It was not difficult for my brothers and sisters to forget I was even there. I became my mother's shadow and her helper. I stayed under her feet. I watched her in the kitchen. It was during this time that I knew I wanted to help others. When my siblings became ill, I would help Mom take care of them. I would carry food or medicine to them on a serving tray. Whatever my mom needed help with, I wanted to help. I was like the chicks that are always at their mother's feet—I felt safe just being near her. I knew my mother had many children, but we knew how deeply she loved each one of us.

In between the times of helping mom or in the quiet of the evening, I found myself lying across my bed talking a lot to this "Lord" whom I had heard so much about while going to church with Robin. I would lay across the bed looking up to the ceiling and talking to Christ. It was at the age of 39 that this Lord began to reveal to me the meaning of the reoccurring dream that gave me the ability to fly and to become invisible.

My ability to become invisible still exists within me, to a certain degree. Instead of physically disappearing, I have become one who remains very introverted, inwardly withdrawn and still easily invisible in a crowd. It would not be until more than three decades later that I would realize through ministry that the invisible child had grown up to become a dead woman walking.

Complete workbook lesson on "The Invisible Child."

4

DEAD WOMAN WALKING

"For the enemy hath persecuted my soul; he hath smitten my life down to the ground; he hath made me to dwell in darkness, as those that have been long dead." Psalm 143:3

In the 42 years following my closet experience, I was like Tamar who lived out the remainder of her dismal existence somewhat exiled in her brother Absalom's house. I displayed all the physical signs of being alive, but in reality, I was a "dead woman walking." Even as I seldom missed a day at work and seemed a permanent fixture at my church, cordially greeting and seating parishioners as an usher, serving in the office of trustee, church nurse, missionary, and Sunday school teacher. Even as I was called to preach the living Word of God, there seemed to be a part of me that was dead. As I look back, I remember trying so hard to have the "religious" experience.

> **I was screaming with my mouth shut. No one heard me.**

Yet as I desperately struggled toward the light, darkness had descended upon my wretched soul, and depression was my daily companion. I was screaming with my mouth shut. No one heard me. It seemed *"the enemy [had] persecuted my soul; he [had] smitten my life down to the ground; he [had] made me to dwell in darkness, as those that [had] been long dead"* (Psalm 143:3).

Were my shouts of joy actually camouflaged cries for relief?

Were my holy dances, in reality, internal wrestling matches between pain and piety? Despite the outward shouting and dancing, I became very adept at ignoring my inward emptiness. As I look back on those days, I realize now that the deceiver was so cunning that he carefully manipulated the Word of God to his advantage. In being a missionary, preacher, and Sunday school teacher, I often misinterpreted certain biblical passages that, in reality, kept me in spiritual bondage. I had suppressed my human feelings so well until I lost my true identity. I had forgotten I was a frightened 4-year-old little girl crying in the dark while masquerading in the body of a smiling 24-year-old woman. The enemy had me so smitten that I resided in a world in which "I" did not really count, for "I" was long since dead.

I had adopted the attitude that as long as everybody else was all right, I had no right not to be fine since one of the real signs of being Holy Ghost-filled was denying what you felt, dismissing your own hurt, and claiming the

$$\left\{ \begin{array}{c} \textbf{I hid myself in plain} \\ \textbf{sight of others.} \end{array} \right\}$$

righteousness of God. Does not Romans 4:17 encourage us to *"calleth those things that which be not as though they were"*? Oh, such a doctrine sounds very pious, but to me, it was really misery turned inside out! Every day was the night of the living dead. The saw the low self-esteem I possessed as a spiritual sign of humility. My refusal to enhance cosmetically my outward appearance was evidence that I had given up worldliness for the riches of glory. My life had become a robotic attempt to live for the Lord while I died to self.

I hid myself in plain sight of others. Every step I took was another step toward oblivion. I was not Yvonne. I was what the hands in the closet made me — a dead woman walking. My mental state was in such disarray that I perceived the executioner (the hands) not as a dreaded foe but rather a dear friend, for he possessed the power, by mere confession, to free me from the prison in which I resided. It was not until ministry that I realized I was not alone and only God possessed the actual power to free me, and thousands of other female inmates like me.

Tori Amos, music artist and co-founder of RAINN (Rape, Abuse and Incest National Network), wrote the following letter:[1]

Dear Friends:

For the past two years, I've sung "Me and a Gun" at every concert as a way of healing the place inside myself that has been hurt, enraged, and numbed by violence. For many years, I shut down that place inside myself that needed to rage, cry, ask questions, and basically just express myself.

I made a conscious choice when I put "Me and a Gun" on the record not to stay a victim anymore. You see, I was still a victim in my own mind from an experience that had happened a long time ago: I was torturing myself. Passion, joy, and love were not things I felt I could have or deserved anymore.

I've been encouraged by wise ones who taught me how to develop inner tools where I can understand these scarred places in my being. It took me many years to make the decision to deal with this, but a bitter woman was what I was becoming, and when I was young, I always saw myself as a passionate woman. I would say, "Well, she's dead," and the wise ones said, "It's your choice, Tori, if you want to bring her back to life, you can. She's only been sleeping—alone, in a very dark corner. It's your choice, and there is help out there."

I received a letter from a 13-year-old girl in Paris whose stepfather has been molesting her for years. She wrote: "If I had known a phone number which would have been able to help me, I certainly would have dialed it."

Healing takes courage, and we all have courage, even if we have to dig a little to find it!

Love and support,
TORI AMOS

By the time you finished reading this letter, according to statistics, another woman was sexually assaulted and entered into the prison that was home to me for 42 years.[2]

> *Every two minutes, a woman is sexually assaulted*

I wanted to share this letter because Amos describes what I was feeling since I identified myself as a dead woman walking. Sexual assault of any kind is a horrible offense to one's person, dignity, self-worth, and pride—to one's entire life.

For the first 42 years of my life, I lay vanquished in a hellacious grave of silence. The peace I found in the silence became my way of life. I rarely spoke unless spoken to. I kept to myself most of the time. Rarely did I reach out to others. I trusted very few people. I dared to share my innermost feelings with any one. My closest sister and I shared a lot during our teenaged years, but I never shared with her or anyone else that I remembered that closet experience. It was as if it never happened. I had convinced myself it was a nightmare. Every time I was confronted with violent acts toward women, children, or men, whether it was watching a movie, the news, or reading a book, I cried.

When I think back over my life, even as a child, I never expressed how I felt about anything. I was afraid! After all, he told me never to tell. If I started talking, would the venomous, volcanic vomit of my victimization spew out? Would I start screaming and never stop? I wasn't sure. I couldn't risk it, so I continued most of my life being an invisible child who now had become a dead woman walking. If someone said something to hurt my feelings, I would just walk away and cry. Consequently, my silence took a toll on my health. As a child, I suffered from severe headaches. I remember having to have a spinal tap done at the age of 11 because the doctors were not sure if I had a brain tumor. The headaches continued into adulthood. Then, I was treated for migraine head- aches. I remember running back and forth to one of the most prestigious clinics in Washington, DC, where my physician prescribed me a pill that was to be taken every five minutes, up to four pills, until the headache subsided.

In my teenage years, writing became the vehicle that transported me from my wretched road of reality to a peaceful path that led to my own paradise. As I grew older, I had no opinions except those that were given to me. I had no voice except the voice of others. I had no acknowledged feelings except those I was given permission to have.

> **Everything from that dark dungeon of a closet was being held in and was literally eating away at me like a terminal, cancerous tumor.**

I married shortly after finishing college, and as a result of the added stress of working my first full time job, adjusting to motherhood, skipping lunch and not hydrating myself, I developed ulcers and lost 20 pounds. My doctor threatened me with hospitalization if I did not start taking better care of myself. Everything from that dark dungeon of a closet was being held in and was literally eating away at me like a terminal, cancerous tumor. I denied myself so much for the sake of others. Even today, I still worry about not inflicting pain on others, no matter what I suffer in the process. But the difference today, as opposed to 42 years ago, is that I know who I am and that I am still a work in progress!

For 42 years, I lived the life of a little girl locked in a closet marked: "Never to be opened." My body grew, but the little girl remained in the closet. Circumstances put me there, but I made a conscious decision to block out and lock within myself that closet experience because of the subconscious fear of resurrecting the pain. Even though the closet was like a grave, like a mausoleum, it oddly had a certain sense of security within it. I saw no urgency or rational reason why I should come out. The truth, however, was that I did not have the faintest notion how to come out of the closet. But thanks be to God, 42 years later, He unlocked that cast iron door through women's ministry. I came face to face with that little girl who had found solace in the prison of the closet for 42 years. I came face to face with that little girl who used to peep through the keyhole, watching her outer-self grow up and make choices. Some choices were not understood until much later in life. Regretfully, most of my life's choices were made within that small, emotional prison.

It was not until I began to know who I was in Christ that I knew the Lord was calling me, as well, to come to Him, take His hand, be healed, and be set free. I could in no way lift up myself. The Lord saw my tears, He heard my cry, and He answered. I contend that our closet issues as women today are (1) innately and spiritually tied to the closet issues of the first woman created and are (2) worsened by the closet issues that resulted as consequences of her part in the fall of mankind. This first woman was just another nameless woman who did not receive an identity until after she was in trouble. She had no idea what she was or who she was.

I contend that our closet issues have risen out of the ghosts of our pasts—ghosts that remain in the closet, no matter what our closet may have been or may be right now. The social principles or morals we were or were not taught and the positive reinforcement of our personhood that was not given in childhood created many of our issues. We became dead women walking because of those who put their hands on our bodies when we were innocent, impressionable children and told us it was okay. Many of our issues were created when our childhood, young adulthood, or womanhood was stolen by the filthy spiders whose hands reached out from the closets, or sneaked into our rooms at night, or came out of nowhere and drug us into alleys or parks, or forced us into cars.

We have become dead women walking because of pain created from our closet experiences of verbal, physical, mental, emotional, social, economic, and spiritual abuse, or mere rejection through the years. Our closet issues have arisen out of being fatherless, having no father in the home, and having no father figure to help validate what we are and who we are. Worse yet, our closet issues have arisen from having absent fathers in the home—they are there, but not *there*. Our closet issues have even arisen out of what we as women were taught by other women about women—you know, how we can't be trusted.

Eve did not have access to women's ministry, but I can almost say with certainty that after the fall, she would have benefited from having another woman with whom she could talk to and relate. I assure you that the ghosts from Eve's past haunted her until her death. Once Adam and Eve fell, Eve entered into a closet of rejection and shame. Not only had her husband blamed her for the sin that had taken place, but her Lord had chastised her for the first time. Eve's beautiful home, the place of her birth, the place where she was given in marriage, the place where she spent many blissful days, was taken from her. Perhaps from this day forward, she remained in her closet of depression, desolation, and despair, and it is my strong belief that Eve died while still in her closet. Today, however, we as women, through the vehicle of ministry, have the opportunity to come out of our closets.

Complete workbook lesson on "Dead Woman Walking."

5

Coming out of the Closet

"Then they cried unto the Lord in their trouble, and he saved them out of their distresses. He brought them out of darkness and the shadow of death, and brake their bands in sunder."
Psalm 107:13-14

"But ye are a chosen generation, a royal priesthood, an holy nation, a peculiar people; that ye should shew forth the praises of him who hath called you out of darkness into His marvelous light."
1 Peter 2:9

Many women like Yvonne grow up never having talked about, more or less, being delivered from the dark, dismal, demons of their past. They grow up physically, but that little girl remains locked inside the closet. Sunday morning service or Bible study are not the places where a woman can deal with herself in the depth she needs to in order to deal with her *self*. She simply, more than likely, will grow up to be just another dead woman walking. Until she deals with *self*, she can never be what God desires her to be. Until she deals with *self*, she can never move toward healing and wholeness.

Unfortunately, as a minister of the Gospel, people think I have it made. People think I have "arrived." Women often look at me as if I do not understand what they are going through simply because I am a minister. People think ministers are exempt somehow from trials and tribulations because of our positions.

The truth of the matter is that we are prime targets for Satan *because* of our calling. I have had many closets from which God has delivered me, and some I still need Him to help me open from the inside so I can walk out and live even the more!

I can identify with Yvonne as a dead woman walking because this is where I was as I began my journey more than 13 years ago. The day I walked through the doors of The Word of God Baptist Church, I discovered the nursery rhyme "Humpty Dumpty"[1] was only partially written. The writer, in my opinion, failed to mention that Humpty possibly had a grandmother, mother, spouse, sister, daughter, aunt, niece, female cousin, and friends who were also shattered into pieces and could not be put back together again by "all of the king's horses and all of the king's men." Mere mortal men will never have the type of healing power that can only come from the Lord.

That day, I felt like I knew much about Humpty's family, if he had a family, because I was one of his nameless sisters. I have realized through women's ministry at The Word of God that there are countless others just like Yvonne and me, countless others whose issues started in, or are still contained in, a closet. Countless others who are broken into a thousand pieces and nothing they have tried has "put them back together again." Humpty's sisters, who were nameless, just like so many of the women in the Bible, had many, many, many issues. In this book, we will come to discuss these issues as "closet issues."

I was a dead woman walking when I first came to The Word of God Baptist Church. I was in what I call a "wilderness experience." I had been suffering from depression for several years. The depression was preempted by my finding out I was pregnant at age 39. I really did not mind my age, but I allowed the adversary to cause me to go into a downward spiral. The adversary taunted me day and night for a while, reminding me my other two children would be grown and out of the nest in a couple of years. Why in the world would I want to start over at this time in my life? If I had an abortion, he said, no one would have to know. I reminded him, however, that it did not matter the costs. If the Lord allowed me to conceive and carry the baby full term, I would have it. Abortion was not an option!

This choice began a downward spiral of depression and rejection. Every day became an awesome, unbelievable chore just to get up in the morning. I felt like I was in a dark tunnel with no light. I was carrying out my daily chores as wife, mother, active member of the church, and boss, yet I was dying inside. I was breathing and moving, yet I was not really alive inside. I was a dead woman walking. The effects of depression can be devastating, destructive, and deadly. (We will address depression in detail in a later chapter.)

I could very much identify with the woman in Luke 13:11, *"And, behold, there was a woman which had a spirit of infirmity eighteen years, and was bowed together, and could in no wise lift up herself."* I had just turned 40 and had to learn to walk all over again after the birth of my son the year before due to a separated pelvis during delivery. The strange thing is that I had no idea just how bent over I was until I began to work in women's ministry. It was so true that I could in no wise lift up myself, but I am so grateful God has the master plan. He is omniscient and knew just what I needed and put His plan into motion. I am so glad I held on to the Master's hand to get me through that closet experience, for my son is one of the greatest joys of my life today.

I had just resigned from a church I had attended for seventeen and a half years the month before I entered the doors of The Word of God Baptist Church. I was a faithful member of that church, held numerous positions, and was called into the preaching ministry there (my calling to ministry goes to show you that God does not call the "superstars"—He just uses ordinary people). However, just like my sister in Luke 13, I came to the temple time after time, broken, bent, and burdened, and no one saw me. No one saw my tears. I really cannot blame the church because I, like so many other women, did the same thing week after week. We come to the house of God weary, wounded, and sad. We say we have given our problem(s) to the Lord, but we drag them back from the altar with us. Sunday after Sunday, we drag that same heavy trunk-load of disappointments, burdens, grief, condemnation, loneliness, and despair. Why, I am not sure. Maybe there is a feeling that since I am a child of God, I should not be feeling this way. Therefore, I have to keep it to myself, or I will be looked down upon or considered "unsaved" or without faith. Unfortunately, many churches do perpetuate this environment, but I am so grateful that Jesus said, *"And ye shall know the truth, and the truth shall make you free"* (John 8:32).

And I became free that miraculous evening in 1998, in the fourth year of the women's ministry at The Word of God as eight women in the ministry class (note that eight is the number of new beginnings) shared their horror stories. That night, the little girl in each of them appeared. When the first woman began to talk about her experience with rape, with tears streaming down her face, it began a domino effect. After the first of the eight finished, the second woman began to share . . . then the third, then the fourth, until all of the women present came face to face with their closet captors.

This was the night my closet captor manifested himself. I could feel his eerie presence. Amidst the maze of the tales of rape, abuse, and feelings of degradation, I could feel the cold hands of my captor again. With memories as real as the pain of the women in that room, he taunted me with the 42-year nightmare of his devilish deeds. At that moment, I realized that as long as I allowed such control over my life, I would remain in that closet forever. I knew as long as I allowed him the safe haven of that dark closet, I, and millions of women like me, would belong to him. I was not willing to concede a lifetime to his dominance. When the reality of that possibility hit me, I knew I had to get out. I felt like the darkness was suffocating me. I could not breathe. I had to get out. I was dying. I was losing my strength like a slow tire leak. Suddenly, I could see a glimpse of light. It was not just a physical light, but The Light, Himself, with outstretched hands, beckoned me to come unto Him. Therefore, with all the energy I could muster, I pushed open the door and did not just come out of the closet, but I ran toward The Light, The Light of Freedom. Now remember, I had been in the ministry classes for four years!

That evening, as I headed home from the women's ministry meeting, I was still reeling from the emotional trauma of having my closet captor return. As I drove down the parkway toward home, my vision was somewhat blurred as my mind was still wandering through the maze of haunted memories of the hands that robbed me of my childhood innocence and purity. The ghoulish memories of 1955-56 seemed to race mercilessly through the dark corridors of 42 years like a horde of frantic and fiendish demons, and again, I became that scared little girl of four years old. This was the day Yvonne appeared. Yvonne was that little girl who was still trapped in, and still peering out of, the closet.

The stories the women shared awakened Yvonne—which so frightened me! I realized that night that my closet captor had risen to the surface, and I, Shirley, was the grown woman who lived outside of the closet. This was the evening I realized Yvonne was Minister Shirley "Yvonne" Cobb, facilitator of the women's ministry at The Word of God Baptist Church, and I needed to do something to get her out of that closet so I could move toward my healing, wholeness, and destiny.

****

Initially, the only way I could deal with the closet experience was to tell it through Yvonne because I was *coming* out of the closet. I was not fully out. I chose to write this first portion of the book using my middle name, Yvonne, because prior to my coming out of my closet of guilt, shame, and despair, I was spiritually trapped. As the first letter of my middle name "Y" is trapped between my first and last name, I, too, felt trapped in the middle between the questions of, *"Was this a dreadful dream, or was this a rude reality?"* I was trapped in the middle of, *"Y did this heinous act happen to ME, and Y did he do this evil thing to ME?"* I was a little girl still trapped in a spiritual closet of the gripping despair that took place in a physical closet of grueling darkness. I was trapped between the burden of bondage and the fullness of freedom. It has taken years to reach the place where I am no longer bound by my past. The Lord has helped me face the truth of my past, and The Truth, Jesus Christ, has made me free!

Many women look at themselves every day in the mirror and have no idea who they really are. We have no idea what our purpose is in this life. We truly have no idea how to love. Because our self-esteem is so low, we really do not know how to love ourselves. Unfortunately, all too often, the same can be said about the men in our lives, but that is the subject of another chapter. Too often, we rush into relationships looking for the other person to make us whole. Only to our sad, heart-broken surprise, we find out that no human being has the power to make us whole because that person might have just as much baggage as we do. T.D. Jakes notes in his book *Woman Thou Art Loosed*[2] that two people enter into a relationship, both only half whole. They think by coming together they can help one another become whole, but this is the only time in a mathematical equation that half + half never equals a whole.

Many of us remain in bondage, bound and gagged, from the horrors of our past. We want to scream but cannot. We want to wake up out of the recurring nightmare, but this never seems to happen. We want to be free but do not know how to get there.

We must come out of our Egypt, out of the closet of our despair, in order to begin the arduous journey to our Canaan—a life bountifully endowed with the succulent grapes of hope and the milk of assurance. Once we come out of the closet, we can truly taste the sweet honey of self-love and know for the first time in our lives who we are and whose we are.

As women, we must come out of the closet in order to experience a physical, emotional, psychological, and most importantly, a spiritual metamorphosis. We must come out of the closet and journey from the darkness and loneliness of a cocoon in order to come into The Light, Jesus Christ, and take flight as the beautiful, fluttering butterfly that God designed us to be.

Until we come out of the closet, we will never experience the abundant and victorious life Jesus said we might have through Him. Until we come out of the closet, we will remain prisoners. To remain prisoners would be to say that Jesus died in vain. Jesus said in Luke 4:18-19,

> *The Spirit of the Lord is on me. He has anointed me to tell the good news to poor people. He has sent me to announce freedom for prisoners. He has sent me so that the blind will see again. He wants me to free those who are beaten down. And he has sent me to announce the year when he will set his people free.* (NIrV)

As women, we first need to identify our closet. Was it an attic, cellar, basement, locker room, bathroom, bedroom, backyard, front yard, alley, parking lot, or the woods? Was it a relationship? Was it a situation created as a result of rape? Was your closet created by the guilt of having an abortion? Did it develop because of abandonment, abuse, or an absent father in the home? Once the closet is identified, we need to know it is okay to come out. Most of us stay in the closet too long because we do not know how to come out, or even that we need to come out. Once we come out, we need to know how to stay out.

Like Maya Angelou, I can say, "Still I rise!" One miraculous night during ministry class, God unlocked the door and ministered to me as I ministered to others. God held my trembling hand and steadied my emotional, wobbling legs. He whispered softly to me and placed reassurance within my soul that it was all right to come out. He said to me, *"As I was with you in your closet, I will be with you when you walk out of that door."*

After 42 years, the little girl, the invisible child, the dead woman walking came out of the dreary darkness of her closet being escorted by the Divine presence of a loving God who ushered her into His marvelous light. In one magnificent, miraculous moment, God ushered me out of the nocturnal agony of that closet experience into the brilliant sunlight of a new beginning. In my case, it took 42 years, but God is never late. He has the master plan, and when things are done in His time, they are done right! However, until the door is opened and that pathetic, pitiful, painful part of us is helped to deal with our closet experiences, we will never be able to move toward healing, wholeness, and our destiny.

Since women are primarily relationship-oriented and we devote much of ourselves to our roles as nurturers, we often lose ourselves in the process. Our relationships with our friends, spouses, and especially with our children, are the primary reasons, I believe, many of us are in closets today. Yes, we contend with the issues of our past, but just as lethal as the demons of our past are the death grips of our present circumstances.

> **But just as lethal as the demons of our past are the death grips of our present circumstances.**

Our relationship with someone may have put us into the closet, but we must make the decision to come out. How long we remain in the closet (whatever our closet may be), depends on the truth of who we are and whose we are. The truth of our identity equips us with the knowledge of our rights. Until we know this, we will not feel we deserve any better. We will not feel we have a right to be free. For so many of us, the depths of who we are and what we can accomplish have not been realized to the fullest. But no matter the obstacle and no matter the challenge, what I have gained through ministry and what you can gain, as well, by coming out of the closet will be surpassed by nothing other than our relationship with the Lord.

Through ministry and my saying, "Enough is enough," and choosing to come out of my closet, my life has taken a bright, beautiful, strong, and positive direction. I have evolved into a self-confident woman of prayer and power. I am secure in who I am and whose I am for the first time in my life. I have come out of Egypt and will never, ever go back. Coming out of the closet has helped me to be the woman God has ordained me to be. No, I have not fully arrived, but watch out, my destiny is within view!

For almost two decades, I have engaged in the tedious task of helping women find their personal key that will allow them an exit from the dark and locked closet into the radiant sunlight of the wondrous seasons of their lives. Ministry and the Word of God can accomplish this, but you will never experience freedom in the fullest until you come out of the closet.

I have dedicated my life to helping women understand that freedom begins with a decision. Women must grasp the reality that we must consciously make the decision to want out so badly that we can envision it, we can almost touch it, we can taste it, and we can all but ingest its fragrance. We must want out so badly that we do more than merely dream about it. We must know our dream can become a reality.

More than 2,000 years ago, Jesus asked a question of a man who had lain by the pool of Bethesda for 38 years. The same question comes down to us, through 2,000 years of history, as we lie awake each night in our pool of tears: "Do you want to be made whole?" If your answer is yes, then women's ministry is for you.

Complete workbook lesson on "Coming out of the Closet."

6

THE NEED FOR MINISTRY

"When Jesus saw him lie, and knew that he had been now a long time in that case, he saith unto him, Wilt thou be made whole?"
John 5:6

Women's ministry is an avenue that helps women learn how to cope with their issues while they are going through them, learn why women are more predisposed to certain issues and what God's Word says about these issues, and learn how to apply the principles of God's Word in their lives to help bring about a resolution. Many mistakenly confuse women's fellowship with women's ministry. Fellowship denotes a coming together for socializing, perhaps to discuss an issue, have refreshments, and go home until the next scheduled event. Fellowship is not ministry. Ministry provides an avenue that truly helps to set the captives free. Ministry is ongoing with some

{ **Fellowship is not ministry.** }

degree of regularity and is structured to create the life-altering experience that is needed for deliverance. Meeting once a month has proven not to be effective in meeting the multitude and severity of issues facing women today. Women need a frequent, ongoing coming together in an established setting to talk, discuss, let go, let God, and be ministered to. We need to know where to find the help to become free and how to remain free. We need to hear the testimonies of others regularly in order to know we are not the only ones going through a particular situation. We need to know we are not alone. Each woman needs to be able to say, unequivocally, "What God has done for others, He can do the same for me!"

Because men pastor most churches in the Christian community,[1] there is a need for women's ministry. I thank God every day for my pastor, Dr. John L. McCoy, who realized the women of The Word of God Baptist Church needed a women's ministry and that the ministry needed to be headed by a woman. I recall Pastor McCoy saying, "I can only do so much for the women because I am not a woman. Nobody knows women better than another woman." Pastor McCoy went on to say, "I counsel them dealing with the issue of rape, but as a man, I cannot fully give the compassion that is needed because I don't know what it is like to be a woman, much less one who has been raped."

In the fall of 1993, after the conclusion of the first class for the men, The Mighty Men's Ministry, headed by Deacon William F. Hulley, Pastor McCoy shared his vision for women's ministry and asked me to organize and facilitate it. Pastor had no idea just how much I needed the ministry. While ministering to others, this ministry would prove to help me truly learn to live. Ministry would help me shake loose the shackles that had me bound and in prison for so long. Ministry would help me evolve from the cold, clammy carcass of a cocoon into the bold, bright, and beautiful butterfly that I am today. Ministry has truly trans- formed my life. In ministry is where I came face to face with the part of me that was trapped and bound in the closet for many years. As I ministered through my own pain, I realized there were countless other women like me. It was in the winter of 1994 that God allowed this vehicle to be born that would help women rise: the Virtuous Women's Ministry (VWM). On February 1, 1994, fourteen brave souls ventured out with me on this journey. They were (in alphabetical order):

1. Brenda Allen (now a deaconess)
2. Marietta Brown
3. Pauline Gilmore (Daniel) (now a deaconess)
4. Beverly Hemsley (now a minister of the Gospel)
5. Annie London (became a facilitator for the ministry and is now assistant executive director of VWM, Inc., also an evangelist)
6. Michele McCoy
7. Ernestine Miles (now a deaconess)
8. Sandra Kedar-Mitchell (became a licensed minister)
9. Minnie Outlaw (now a deaconess)
10. Hannah Berry Petteway (became a facilitator in charge of the VWM in North Carolina and is now an ordained minister)
11. Maria Pugh (my sister, became a facilitator for the Little Girls' Ministry class)
12. Helen Robinson (my sister, now works with the women's ministry at another church and is a deaconess)
13. Mother Lillie M. Young (my mother, became a facilitator-in-training for the Women of Wisdom ministry)
14. Sheila Young (my sister-in-law, became a minister's wife and deaconess)

These women, when they came into the ministry, were dealing with many issues in their lives. My mother, at the conclusion of the sessions, at the age of 60, learned how to be good to herself for the first time in her life. Having raised 10 children, all of the resources went toward food, clothing, and shelter, of course. As long as we had what we needed as children, mom was satisfied, but through this ministry, she learned it was all right to do something for herself without guilt. In May of 1994, these women completed the first phase of the ministry class. As my mother marched in with the others, my heart was overjoyed with pride, as she and the other women had moved a little closer to becoming healed and whole.

Why is women's ministry needed? At least 70 to 85 percent of churches are comprised of women.[2] If 50 percent of the 70 to 85 percent suffer from low self-esteem and are bound by issues from their past, this is a tremendous hindrance to church growth, personal growth, and spiritual growth and a hindrance in fulfilling God's purpose in the lives of His children. This most certainly cripples the vision of the pastor.

> **Women's ministry is not the answer to every issue, but it is a beginning.**

The church may be considered a "hospital for the sick," but at some point, the sick must move toward healing and wholeness to make room for the others who come in as we fulfill the Great Commission: *"Go ye therefore, and teach all nations . . . Teaching them to observe all things whatsoever I have commanded you"* (Matthew 28:19, 20). The Word says, *"We then that are strong ought to bear the infirmities of the weak, and not to please ourselves"* (Romans 15:1). How can we bear any of our sisters' infirmities if we are never strong enough? We must be at a certain spiritual level to witness to others. We cannot fulfill God's purpose for our lives if we remain burdened, bound, and buried by past hurts, past shames, and past failures in relationships. If we remain heavy-laden by whatever put us in the closet, we will never be the women God has called us to be.

Ministry helps young girls and women identify their closets and helps them understand why they must come out of the closet. Ministry equips them with what they need in order to come out of the closet. Ministry teaches girls and women how to live once they come out, provides the love and support they need to help them stay out, and helps prevent them from going into another one. As women, we must come out of the closet in order to experience true freedom in Christ.

Unfortunately, many of us have suffered unnecessarily for years because we did not have access to ministry. However, it is through ministry that we can rise from the unmarked grave of obscurity, the unmarked grave of invalidation, and the unmarked grave of invisibility. Through ministry, women can rise from the life-long, hellacious grips of no and low self-esteem, rise from the degrading stigma of having our identity defined by the sizes and shapes of our anatomy, and rise from being validated only by the sir name of our spouse or by the successes and failures of our children. We can rise from the humiliating label of "divorcee" or the "scarlet letter" of being caught in the act of adultery, rise from having our value diminished because of giving birth to a life without benefit of a wedding ring, and rise from our long, bitter seasons of winter.

Ministry can help give countless women hope when they feel no one understands. Women who have suffered or are still suffering from the gut-wrenching hurt and torture of their past and present circumstances will know they can be delivered and set free through ministry. Ministry can help usher those who remain in the dark, dismal, dungeon of their closet out into the radiant realm of reality and let them know there is nothing too hard for God. Women need to know there is life after tragedy, life after abortion, life after drugs, life after divorce, life after abandonment, life after rape, life after alcoholism, life after adultery, life after prostitution, life after homosexuality, and life after abuse.

Regardless of what put us in the closet, we can come out with victory because of Christ. We can live! Jesus said in John 10:10: *"The thief cometh not, but for to steal, and to kill, and to destroy: I am come that they might have life, and that they might have it more abundantly."* We do not have to remain dead women walk. We can be delivered from the nightmares, the horrors, and the heinous, unmentionable things that have remained hidden and tightly locked in the closet for all of these years. This was definitely good news for me.

Most importantly, ministry provides an avenue for HEALING. Ministry is needed to give hope while in the

Helps women who have been damaged physically, emotionally, morally, spiritually, and economically move toward wholeness

Empowers women to rise out of feelings of hopelessness and despair

Addresses strongholds so women can start living in the present in order to have a successful future

Lifts women suffering from low self-esteem and depression as a result of being victimized by society

Inspires women to excel in their homes, work, and worship places because they realize they are no longer victims, but victors in Christ

Nourishes and strengthens relationships among women and helps them to feel better about themselves, moving them toward wholeness, therefore creating stronger membership and a greater support of the leader's vision in churches and other organizations

Guides women to higher levels of spiritual growth through God's Word

valley of despair and to give guidance out of the valley of the shadow of death. Some women need to know their struggle is not a sign of insanity and they are not the only ones who feel the way they do. Ministry is needed to help women know we are special and we matter. We come together in ministry to learn our identity, to discover our purpose in life, to share our problems and issues, to be uplifted by one another, and to learn we are not the only ones bearing our particular crosses. As we study God's Word in ministry and draw nigh unto Him, He reminds us that what He has done for others, He will do the same for us. *"Jesus is the same yesterday, to day, and for ever"* (Hebrews 13:8, NKJV).

Ministry helps to teach, instruct, give hope, and encourage women so we are able to stand and say that we are:

More than conquerors

Ingeniously created by God, fearfully and wonderfully made

No longer a victim but a victor in Christ

Innately free to forgive

Sealed unto the day of redemption

Transformed

Royalty, and

Yoked together with other sisters

And we are:

Made by the mighty hands of God

Inspired because I am who God says I am

Never alone

Innately forgiven

Set free by the Son

Tried by the fire

Redeemed by the blood of Christ, and

Yielding self daily to the will of God

In ministry, I have seen God deliver women from low or no self-esteem and from the bowels of fornication and adultery to forgiveness of self and forgiveness of others. Ministry has freed many from the grips of bitterness and anger. Through ministry, God has healed physical, emotional, and spiritual maladies. I have seen God break the binds of the enemy which had women, young and old, guilt-ridden because of divorce, broken relationships, and abortions that may have happened five, ten, or twenty years ago.

No single ministry session can ever "fix" one's life. However, ministry is a vehicle that can help women move closer to The One who can put us back together again. Women's ministry is not the answer to every issue, but it is a beginning.

Through women's ministry, I have seen women rise up for the first time in their lives and say: "I do matter; I do count." Through women's ministry, I have seen young girls and women refuse to be used anymore as mere sex objects. In women's ministry, many women, just as I, for the first time in their lives, will not only come out of the closet but will also rise in victory over that closet experience. And as we are coming out of the closet, we can begin to answer the question, "Who am I?"

Complete workbook lesson on "The Need for Ministry."

7

WHO AM I?

"I will praise thee: for I am fearfully and wonderfully made: marvelous are Thy works" Psalm 139:14

I have often asked myself the ultimate questions, "Who am I?" "What is my true identity?" I have longed to know who I was born to be before those damning days in that suffocating closet. Who did God create me to be before my future was determined by the mind behind those perverted hands? Those perverted hands that scarred my self-image and shut my mouth for 40 years. What silly memorable statements would I have blurted out in my adolescence that would still give my parents an opportunity for laughter? What profound statements would I have uttered in high school that would have given my teachers reason to believe I was destined for some Ivy League institution? I wonder, even to this hour, what I would have become if my lips were not so tightly sealed by fear and guilt that I ceased to ever really speak for most of my childhood and the first decade and a half of my adult life.

> These are the days when every fiber within me is screaming, "Who am I? Will the real me please stand up!"

I wake up morning after morning, and I look in the mirror as I prepare for the day. There are some mornings when I look at the person looking back at me and say, *"I am woman . . . hear me roar! I am confident, compassionate, and content with my life and myself."* I can say on these days, *"Girl, you got it going on!"* Then, there are other days when I look into the eyes of that person who is staring back at me and ask, *"Who are you, and what do you want from me?"* On these days, I wonder *who* and *what* I have to be that day. Shall I be wife, mother, housekeeper, seamstress, nurse, gardener, car pool mother, den mother, grocery shopper, errand runner, kisser-of-the-children's-ouches and bed-tucker-in-er? *"Why do I have to be these things today!"* It is on these days that I have neither the energy nor the strength to jump through hoops and leap over walls. My mind becomes cloudy and complex trying to figure out how I am going to accomplish all the things I need to do that day, and it never helps when everyone is pulling at me and wants a piece of me before I even get out of the house. God already has given me strength to make it through the night. Now, day has come, and I find myself praying and asking God to give me the strength to make it through the next hour, much less the whole day. These are the days when

> **There are many women inside of me, and the situation mostly determines which woman will show up.**

every fiber within me is screaming, *"Who am I? Will the real me please stand up!"*

As a woman, I know I am not alone. In my opinion, the many facets of what is required of us as women, along with our chemical makeup, almost lends itself to a type of multiple personality. I know there are many women inside of me, and the situation mostly determines which woman will show up.

Cynthia Hicks, co-author of *The Feminine Journey: Understanding the Biblical Stages of a Woman's Life*,[1] details what she believes are the six stages of a woman:

(1) **The Creational Woman**

She is also known as Adam. This stage ranges from puberty (approximately age 12) to age 18. In this stage, the woman struggles primarily with self-esteem.

(2) **The Young Woman**

She is physically grown and usually between the ages of 18 and 30. In this stage, the woman has discovered that her beauty is a very powerful tool.

(3) **The Nurturing Woman**

As far as age is concerned, the nurturing woman overlaps with the young woman. In this stage, the woman embraces the pain and joys of womanhood.

(4) **The Relational Woman**

In this stage, the woman celebrates rather than denigrates gender differences. She appreciates the fact that men are men and women are women.

(5) **The Wounded Woman**

Wounded women are generally women who are divorced, or widowed, or women who have been victimized by childhood trauma.

(6) **The Woman of Strength**

This woman is approaching the end of her journey. She is a teacher of wisdom and is akin to the Titus 2 woman who teaches the younger women how to be chaste and discreet. She is a teacher of good things.

It is important to understand that with the exception of the creational woman and the young woman, the rest of these stages may not occur necessarily in this order. Since the remaining stages may not occur in order, I believe we can be any or all of these women at the same time, depending on what situation arises. We may be chronologically past a particular stage, but if we do not address certain problems that occurred during that stage, we can be mentally, emotionally, and spiritually in limbo and unable to embrace all the next stage has to offer. I believe the experiences that may occur during these six stages can result in any of the following personalities. I describe these personalities as Fill-in-the-Blank Felicia, Depressed Diana, and Lonely Lydia.

Fill-in-the-blank Felicia

When you are asked to introduce yourself, do you begin with a title? If you are like most women, you probably do. "I am Jamie's mother." "I am Deaconess Kelso." "I'm Mary's grandmother," or "Peter's wife." You are not alone. As women, we wear so many hats that we identify ourselves based on these hats or titles. Before ministry, I really had very little knowledge of "what I was," never mind "who I was." It was through ministry that I discovered that I am woman, first, before I am anyone or anything else. Before wife or mother, I am woman! Why did it take me so long to realize this?

Social theorists Impett and Peplau assert that women are more relationship-oriented than men.[2] From the very beginning of time, we can see how women have associated their identities with relationships. We can begin with the first woman, Eve.

Even though Eve did not know who she was as a woman, she knew she was in a relationship, and that is how she identified herself. Until she became a mother, Eve had no real identity, except that of Adam's wife. When we look at Genesis 3:1-2, we find the serpent talking to the woman:

> *Now the serpent was more subtil than any beast of the field which the Lord God hath made. And he said to the woman, Yea, hath God said, <u>Ye</u> shall not eat of every tree of the garden?*
> (The first words ever spoken by the woman) *And the woman said unto the serpent, <u>We</u> may eat of the fruit of the trees of the garden.* (emphasis added)

We as women usually identify ourselves in relation to the roles we fulfill. We naturally offer that information as an appendage to who we are. You very seldom hear a man, when asked who he is, give the roles he fulfills. Usually the male response is: "Hi, my name is Frank." They wait to be asked another question before they tell people what they do or any information about their families.

However, because women are relationship-oriented and nurturers, we devote ourselves totally to our roles and often lose ourselves in the process, if we are not careful. One of the main fill-in-the-blank roles we often lose ourselves in is that of wife, and when we look back, perhaps we see signs of losing our identity long before the walk down the aisle.

> Women should think twice about saying, "I do," and even more about to whom they say it. Lies at the altar need not be ignored.

On May 9, 2006, Oprah's show aired a program that dealt with women who were getting cold feet 30 to 90 days prior to their wedding day. Dr. Robin Smith, a guest psychologist, introduced her book *Lies at the Altar*,[3] in which she addresses the issue of women who ignore the unexplained feelings they have prior to their wedding day. Often, she explains, women enter into marriage under the notion that it is their job to make someone else happy, that it is their job, after they are married, to shrink away— to lose their identity. Dr. Smith notes, "Shrinking women don't make good wives." No matter how noble we may think it is to "totally deny ourselves for the sake of our husbands." I believe this denial creates an underlying anger within us that causes many issues, some of which we will address in a later chapter. Too frequently, women come to equate marriage with becoming non-existent.

Let's think about this for a moment. On the topic of marriage, the Bible mentions several times the idea of two becoming one flesh. Do we as ministers and pastors mislead people as to the real meaning of "Til death us do part" in wedding vows? This does not mean until we literally kill each other. But what happens too often is that we do kill each other, slowly, day after day, year after year, by chipping away at one another's soul until we both end up "dead"—even if we remain in the relationship.

> **Too frequently, women come to equate marriage with becoming non-existent.**

Kristin Armstrong, who was a guest on the Oprah show that day and married to a famous personality, made this statement: "The warden was pride, and I was in maximum security." She talked about trying to be everything to everybody while being too prideful or afraid to say, "I can't do this all by myself" or "I'm just plain too tired!" Armstrong later stated, "Marriage has the potential to erode the very fiber of your identity." For this reason alone women should think twice about saying, "I do," and even more about to whom they say it. Lies at the altar need not be ignored. Neither should lies *after* the altar!

Depressed Diana

Not feeling well and don't know why? Do you have a lack of energy? Are you experiencing trouble concentrating and making decisions? Do you have feelings of helplessness? Do you often ask yourself, "What's the use?" "What does it matter anyway?" Have you lost interest in activities you once enjoyed? Are you unable to sleep or feel like sleeping all the time? Not interested in eating or want to eat all of the time? If you are experiencing any of these symptoms, you very well may be suffering from depression like Diana.

There are certain conditions or illnesses that women are more susceptible to than men. Depression is at the top of the list. On average, rates of depression are twice as high in women as they are in men.[4] Studies have shown that these relative differences are consistent across cultures, despite the variation within and between countries.[5] In other words, regardless of our race, nationality, culture, or socioeconomic status, depression does not discriminate. Studies also show that 1 in 5 women may experience a depressive episode at some point during their lives.[6] From puberty to menopause, women are more susceptible to depression.[7] Think about this: from puberty to menopause—*this is the woman's entire lifespan!*

Lonely Lydia

Have you ever been so lonely you just wanted to die? So lonely you truly had no desire to keep on breathing? Someone reading this right now may say, "Lydia, don't be so melodramatic!" Well, you can say that because you have never been there, and I pray for your sake that if you have never experienced loneliness to this level, you never will. But I know, too well, that many reading this right now are either (1) remembering that deep, soulful, gut-wrenching experience not so long ago or are (2) *living*, but in reality are dead women walking—faking it every second of the day, just trying to make it through.

Every day I awakened, I was trying to figure out how I would make it through that day, much less the night. I dreaded the night, rather the stillness of the night. It seemed so endless at times. The dark seemed to embrace the loneliness, empower my depression, and almost exclude me from humanity. No human should ever have to experience loneliness to this extent.

You lie awake many nights watching each hour go by on the clock. TICK . . . TICK . . . TICK. It's 1 a.m. Then it's 2 a.m. Then you look over at the clock and it's 3 a.m. You lie there longing for dawn to come because you can't take the darkness much longer. This is a great night because perhaps you are dozing off during the seconds before the next hour arrives, versus your worst nights in which you literally see 1 a.m. . . . 1:01 a.m. . . . 1:02 a.m. . . . and on and on and on. These are the nights when you really do not know if you closed your eyes at all. The loneliness grips you so much until it seems to choke the life out of you. And if the Lord— yes, the Lord—were not holding you in the hollow of His hands, you would have swallowed more than just one sleeping pill and ended it all, opposed to living with the deadness of loneliness for what seems like forever. You hear that men often cry in the dark because, as men, they feel they dare not cry openly. However, there is nothing as sad as a woman, especially a married one, who lies beside her husband night after night crying in the dark because she is lonely!

There is a difference between being lonely at times and suffering from loneliness. Loneliness is a type of emotional, psychological, and spiritual grave. Outside of our relationship with God, there is no

> Loneliness is a type of emotional, psychological, and spiritual grave.

perfect solution to dealing with loneliness. Suicide is never the answer because it leaves victims behind. Staying busy during the day to help the time to pass, working on a project at night until it's time to "let Calgon take us away," becoming so exhausted that we just fall into bed, watching TV, or reading until we can't keep our eyes open are only temporary solutions. Accomplishing some lifelong dream, at best, will only bring about some measure of self-fulfillment. Going back to school and travelling to exotic places are pacifying pit stops, but they do not land us on the shores of our utopian destination of authentic, spiritual fulfillment. We must utilize our time to enhance our relationship with the Lord as never before, especially those who are single.

> I dreaded the night, or rather the stillness of the night. It seemed so endless at times. The dark seemed to embrace the loneliness, empower my depression, and almost exclude me from humanity.

Communing with God through reading, studying His word, meditation, prayer, and praise will ultimately give birth to the fulfillment that enhances all other human relationships.

****

Before ministry, I did not know all of these women existed inside of me. I was overwhelmed with emotion, but I did not know what I was feeling, why I was feeling it, or why I would feel a certain way during a particular situation. I recall vividly the first ministry class held in 1994. The first lesson was "Who Am I?" This is where I sensed God desired for us to begin our journey. Confirmation came as the participants began to share what they had written. One of the women in the class, as she began to share what she had written, burst into tears. She stated that she called her sister and asked her sister who she was because she could not answer the question herself. For most women who do not have the benefit of ministry, they never come to the realization of who they really are and their purpose in this life. Often, many of us are of the mindset that because we are not classified as the *head*, then we are the *tail*.

Unfortunately, many churches are still perpetuating this type of mindset today, in the 21st century, that women are a minority and are, and forever will be, second-class citizens. I consider this a travesty against the nature of God Almighty because it discriminates against God's people based on gender, in the very house of God.

In ministry meetings, we start the "Who Am I?" lesson by having women share who they think they are. We give them no further instructions except that there is no page limit. Before the ministry course concludes, we revisit this topic under another heading to see if their opinions about who they are have changed.

When we as women come into the knowledge of who we are according to the Word of God, there is a tremendous rise in self-esteem, and when our self-esteem increases, we feel special. We feel like we are somebody, simply because God says we are. When our self-esteem increases, the lives of those around us are happier. There is more peace within the home because there is greater peace within us. When our self-esteem increases, we realize we are neither the head nor the tail and realize we have no need to be either. We are satisfied with being the helpmeet (not just in the role as wife). Moreover, as helpers, we must be as strong as, if not stronger, than those whom we are called upon to help. When our self-esteem increases, we no longer allow ourselves to be walked upon like a doormat. When our self-esteem increases, we truly can love others because we know how to, and we are comfortable loving ourselves. When our self-esteem is strong, then we can move toward fulfilling God's purpose for our lives. When our self-esteem is strong, we can be the help God desires us to be to our pastors and churches. We move from a position of being a part of the problem to being a part of the solution. Make no mistake, there will still be days when we feel as depressed as Diana, days when we are waiting for that blank to be filled like Felicia, and days when we are as

> **When our self-esteem increases, we realize we are neither the head nor the tail and realize we have no need to be either. We are satisfied with being the helpmeet (not just in the role as wife).**

lonely as Lydia. But the good news is that these personalities will no longer define who we are.

****

POSITIVE AFFIRMATIONS

Each time we come together in our ministry classes, we ask each woman to use a positive affirmation to describe herself, using the first letter in her first name. For instance, my name is Shirley. I would say, my name is "sensational" Shirley or "seeking" Shirley, etc., *"For as [she] thinketh in [her] heart, so is [she]"* (Proverbs 23:7, feminine emphasis mine). If we do not think well of ourselves, if we do not think that we are somebody, and if we do not think we are special and that we have a right to be treated as special, then why should anyone else feel that way about us?

SCRIPTURE MEMORIZATION

The second thing we ask participants to do is commit scripture to memory. This is crucial because we cannot always pull out our Bibles everywhere we go, nor do we always have our Bibles with us. Committing scripture to memory is vital because if God's Word is not in us, then how can we walk according to His Word (Psalm 119:105)? If we do not know His Word, how can we pray His Word in our specific situations? For this reason, we need to hide the Word in our hearts as David declared (Psalm 119:11), not only so we may not sin against God but also because when situations arise, God can bring back to our remembrance what His Word says. How can something be brought back to remembrance if it has never been read, seen, or heard?

SELF-EDIFICATION

The third thing that we do after devotion at the opening of each session is tell what we have done for ourselves since the last time we were together. It is extremely important in increasing self-esteem to know and feel you have self-worth, to know you deserve to be treated special simply because of who you are. Keep in mind that being good to yourself does not always involve spending money. You may decide to read that book that you have wanted to read for a long time, take a walk, spend quiet time with yourself, or on occasion, instead of a shower, let Calgon take you away! You could even use candles and plenty of bubbles! Learn to relax. Learn to "Selah."[8]

In chapter four of St. John, Jesus met a woman of Samaria at Jacob's well who was in search of the answer to the question, "Who am I?" I believe her identity was tied to the men in her life. This nameless woman had no idea who she was, embodying the characteristics of Fill-in-the-blank Felicia, Depressed Diana, and certainly Lonely Lydia. I believe this nameless woman felt she was nobody without a man in her life, jumping into relationship after relationship. Perhaps this is why she had five husbands, and the one she was living with when she met Jesus was not hers. We deal with this woman in the video produced by the ministry entitled *Your Date with Destiny*. This woman had a date with destiny ordained before the foundation of the world. Jesus knew where she would be at that very second. This is why Jesus needed to go through Samaria (St. John 4:4). Jesus met her to confront her, to tell her what she needed to know in order to discover who she was for the first time in her life. It was her date with destiny! It was her day to be set free.

Complete workbook lesson on "Who Am I?"

8

HE CAME TO SET THE CAPTIVES FREE

"If thou shalt confess with thy mouth the Lord Jesus, and shalt believe in thine heart that God hath raised him from the dead, thou shalt be saved." Romans 10:9

You may be wondering how this title fits into helping women come out of the closet in their lives. Simple. Until we know Jesus for ourselves, not just know *about* Him, but truly *know* Him, we will forever remain prisoners. Not just prisoners to sin, but prisoners to our past, present, or future. Before we accept Christ into our lives, we are, in the truest sense, spiritually dead women walking!

We can also be spiritually dead because of those things that continue to hold us captive, those painful closet experiences that keep us shackled, sometimes for years. We have all had closet experiences. Whether our closet experiences were a result of what we did or what was done to us, we each can recall the painful memories. While our closet experiences may have been different, we can find some common similarities in the results of them. Do you think you are not worthy of God's salvation? Do you feel unworthy of God's grace? Do you feel you have done something that is unforgiveable? Do you think you will never be able to forgive the person who caused you horrendous pain? The blessed hope for everyone is that regardless of our answers to these questions, Jesus came to set the captives free.

Too often, we have a difficult time forgiving ourselves and walking in God's forgiveness when we have done something wrong. We feel unworthy of God's forgiveness and hold ourselves captive for days, months, and even years, and we do not experience the fulfillment that God has for our lives. Paul reminds us in God's Word that *"All have sinned, and come short of the glory of God"* (Romans 3:23). No one is exempt from sin. No matter how hard we may try not to, we all have done and will do things that are not pleasing in God's sight. Romans 7:18-19 (NIV) reminds us that nothing good dwells in the flesh. Paul honestly explains, *"For what I do is not the good I want to do; no, the evil I do not want to do—this I keep on doing"* (19). Nevertheless, thanks to God, we can be forgiven for the wrong deeds we commit. For He tells us in 1 John 1:9 that if we would just confess our sins, He is faithful and just to forgive us of these sins and cleanse us from all unrighteousness. We can receive forgiveness for the sins we have committed! Nothing, and I do mean nothing (outside of rejecting God's gift of grace through Jesus Christ, which is a form of blasphemy against the Holy Spirit), is unforgiveable (Luke 12:10)! As long as we confess our sin, we are forgiven and should then repent from it and walk in God's grace.

God's ultimate form of grace, salvation, is offered to all who believe in His Son, Jesus Christ: *"But God commendeth his love toward us, in that, while we were yet sinners Christ died for us"* (Romans 5:8). John says, *"God so loved the world [us], that he gave his only begotten Son, that whosoever believeth in him should not perish, but have eternal life"* (3:16). That is good news!

Many of us also have closet experiences due to some wrong that was done to us. This may be something so painful from which we have never recovered. It may hurt so much that the mere mention or even the thought of it sends us through an indescribable mental anguish. If you do not remember anything else, please remember: *What was done to you was not your fault!* What child could defend herself against older people? What person, young or old, could defend himself against a gang or against a weapon? Unfortunately, people are victimized every day. Much to our sorrow, evil was loosed the day sin was committed in the garden, which caused all of us to be born in sin and shapened in iniquity. This is why mankind can commit such violent acts against others with seemingly no conscience. Sin created the sick, fiendish minds of our perpetrators, and sometimes we want to seek revenge upon those who have hurt us. However, Proverbs 24:29a (NKJV) offers us this wise counsel, *"Do not say, 'I will do to him just as he has done to me.'"* As much as we may feel justified in doing so, as Christians, we know this is not what God would have us to do. We must leave the consequences for the injustices done toward us in the hands of the Almighty God.

> **We must leave the consequences for the injustices done toward us in the hands of the Almighty God.**

Paul admonishes us in Romans 12:17, 19, and 21 (NKJV), *"Repay no one evil for evil"*; *"Beloved, do not avenge yourselves, but rather give place to wrath; for it is written, 'Vengeance is Mine, I will repay,' says the Lord"*; *"Do not be overcome by evil, but overcome evil with good."*

God also admonishes us to forgive those who have wronged us. Forgive them? This is often a very painful pill to swallow. Forgiving others when they have wronged us, especially intentionally, is one of the most difficult things for many of us to do. However, we have no idea the magnitude of closet captivity we place ourselves in when we do not forgive others. The pain of what they have done to us, coupled with our unforgiveness of them, can often become a stronghold from which only God can loose.

Whether your closest experience is a result of what you have done or what someone has done to you, Jesus came that we might be free, that we might have and experience life abundantly. We find Jesus' mission written by the Prophet Isaiah in chapter 61, verses 1-2, but in the Gospel of Luke, chapter 4, verses 18-19, Jesus proclaims His own mission:

> 'The Spirit of the Lord is on me, because I am marked out by him to give good news to the poor; he has sent me to make well those who are broken-hearted; to say that the prisoners will be let go, and the blind will see, and to make the wounded free from their chains, To give knowledge that the year of the Lord's good pleasure is come.' (BBE)

Once we become a child of God, Christ's mission becomes our mission. The "me" becomes "you," and it becomes our responsibility to do these things. Once we accept Jesus as our personal Savior, we can break down this passage, put it into the proper perspective, and answer the questions in the workbook exercise for this chapter:

✜ Who are the poor?

✜ Who are the brokenhearted?

✜ Who are the captives?

✜ Whose sight needs to be recovered?

✜ Who must be set free?

✜ Who are the bruised?

✜ What does it mean to preach the acceptable year of the Lord?

✜ Not everyone is called to preach in the traditional sense (from the pulpit); therefore, how do you fulfill this mission?

****

In the Bible, we have several accounts of salvation coming to women after they were delivered from physical, emotional, and spiritual illnesses. We must understand that until we first know Christ in the pardon of our sins, there can be no real freedom. Look at the following situations that involved women in the Bible.

Luke 8:1-3 reads:

> *And it came to pass afterward, that he went throughout every city and village, preaching and shewing the glad tidings of the kingdom of God: and the twelve were with Him, And certain women, which had been healed of evil spirits and infirmities, Mary called Magdalene, out of whom went seven devils, And Joanna the wife of Chuza, Herod's steward, and Susanna, and many others, which ministered unto him of their substance.*

These women had emotional, physical, and spiritual issues. However, it is of great significance that the three women who were mentioned by name, as well as the others, once delivered, gave out of the abundance of their substance and became devoted, dedicated followers of Jesus. In addition to the three women above who were called by name, I believe the three nameless women listed below also ministered and gave of their substance after their deliverance.

THE WOMAN WITH THE ISSUE OF BLOOD

We do not know how much the woman with the issue of blood for 12 years knew about Jesus prior to her deliverance, but we do know that she knew enough to believe that if she could just touch His clothes, she would be delivered. It is recorded in both Matthew 9:21 and Mark 5:28, *"For she said within herself, If I may but touch his garment, I shall be whole."*

WOMAN CAUGHT IN THE ACT OF ADULTERY

As recorded in the Gospel of John, chapter 8, verse 7, Jesus said to the Pharisees who wanted to stone to death the woman who was caught in the act of adultery, *"He that is without sin among you, let him first cast a stone at her."* As Jesus stooped to write on the ground, only the woman remained. Her accusers dropped their stones and, one by one, walked away. When Jesus stood He said: *"'Woman, where are those thine accusers? hath no man condemned thee?' She said, 'No man, Lord.' And Jesus said unto her, 'Neither do I condemn thee: go, and sin no more'"* (10-11). I believe this woman received Jesus that day, followed Him from that moment forward, and was among the women at the foot of the cross at Calvary.

WOMAN WITH THE SPIRIT OF INFIRMITY

The woman in Luke 13:11 who had a spirit of infirmity for 18 years gives us another very important reason why deliverance is crucial. Some scholars believe this woman was already saved.

What she teaches us is that our deliverance does not lie in isolating ourselves and wallowing in self-pity. Our deliverance lies in continuing to put our service to God first, no matter what. This woman's deliverance may have come after 18 years, but it came. And for her, it came right in the house of God!

****

Contemporary women whose testimonies have touched me insofar as their coming out of their closets:

Mrs. Lillie Mae Young

My mother, who raised ten children. All of her life, she sacrificed her identity until she came into the ministry at the age of 60 and discovered she was more than just a mother, she was a woman, first. It was in the ministry class that Momma learned her self-worth. She learned it was okay to do special things for herself.

Frances Jones

President of our Deaconess Ministry and now author of five books. She is a nationally renowned deaconess extraordinaire whose closet brought her to Washington, DC, 45 years ago on a train with two children and $24 in her pocket.

Sharon McGilvery

A participant of several ministry classes who overcame unbelievable mental and emotional strongholds in her life. It was through ministry that she grew from having no self-esteem to realizing she was not the sum total of a broken relationship. It was in ministry that she discovered she was truly God's beautiful masterpiece and deserved to be happy and free.

A woman who was abandoned and left with two little boys to raise (one of whom was my pastor). Raising her children in the church, she instilled in them a love for God and a high degree of self-confidence. Mrs. McSwain remained the ultimate virtuous woman and was found by Norman McSwain, her soul mate.

****

A woman's relationship with the Lord can bring her through some unbelievable closet experiences. The women who followed Jesus never left Him. They followed Him everywhere He went, even to Calvary and to the tomb. On that dreadful day, as they watched their Savior being brutally beaten, tormented, and nailed to a cross, blood streaming down his face and blood pouring from His hands, His side, and His feet, I know their hearts were breaking. They witnessed the torment of the One who looked beyond all of their faults, delivered them from demons, and healed their broken bodies and messed-up minds. The One who healed their sin-sick souls, the One who forgave them for adultery, the One who loved them unconditionally without asking for anything, the One who set them free. Surely, they were in great despair as they experienced the agonizing torture of their Savior slowly being torn away from them; it must have seemed as if their hearts were being ripped out of their bodies and as if their lives were ending. It must have appeared as if all hope was lost.

As the women stood and watched until their Savior took His last shallow breath, until their Lord was gone, I imagine they were shaken, shattered, and in shock. However, as devastated as they had to have been watching His life end, their love for Him still prevailed. If they could have taken Him down from the cross and immediately carried His lifeless body to the cold tomb, I believe they would have. However, because of Jewish custom, they had to wait until after the Sabbath to go prepare His body for burial. So, on the day after the Sabbath, early in the morning, some of these women were the first to arrive at the tomb of their Lord. Why? Because of their love.

Oftentimes, women feel their relationship with Christ is the only unconditional relationship they have (I am sure some men feel the same way). The closest we come to unconditional love in a relationship outside of the Lord is with our children. In most of our relationships, people love us *because of*. But we know nobody can love us *in spite of* like the Lord.

If Christ could deliver a woman from multiple demons, a woman who had emotional issues, a woman with physical issues who became a pauper as a result of her illness, and a woman caught in the act of adultery, then He can deliver you! If Christ could deliver women who have had to raise their children alone, women who have experienced physical, mental, verbal, and socioeconomic abuse, women who have been tied up, raped, and left for dead, women who have had no self-esteem, and a woman trapped in a closet for 42 years, then He can deliver you! This is what grace is all about. Grace is unmerited, undeserved favor.

The dispensation of GRACE was ushered in at Calvary.
At Calvary, Jesus became the:

> **G**rave robber—*who*
> **R**edeemed us—*and now*
> **A**ccepts us for who we are
> **C**ancelled the penalty of sin—*and offers us*
> **E**ternal life

No matter how "bad" you think you may be, no matter how "dirty" you may think you are, no matter how "crazy" people may think you are or if you feel you are losing your mind, no matter how many times you have been told you are nothing and no one wants you, no matter what habit you may have had or are still struggling with, Jesus said, *"Come unto me."* Even if you are still drinking, using drugs, prostituting yourself, or in an adulterous affair, just *"Come unto me"* (Matthew 11:28)!

My pastor has shared his testimony with us many times, how he had been contemplating suicide before he surrendered his life to the Lord. The moment before he pulled the trigger, he remembered the words his mother told him as he was growing up: "When you don't know what to do, call on the Lord!" So, he called on the Lord, and the Lord said to him, "Since you are ready to throw your life away, give it Me." He was called into the ministry, and more than 30 years later, he is still preaching the gospel. Jesus came to set the captives free!

No matter what state you are in, JUST COME!

COME *with your broken heart!*
COME *being broken in spirit!*
COME *even though you feel you are on the verge of losing your mind!*
COME *with your tear-stained face!*
COME *with unclean hands!*
COME *if you feel heaven doesn't want you and even hell won't take you! There is no time to waste!*
COME *to Jesus just as you are!*

If you are reading this text and have not received Christ, you should give your life to the Lord today, for tomorrow may be too late. Paul writes in Romans 10:9, *"That if thou shalt confess with thy mouth the Lord Jesus, and shalt believe in thine heart that God hath raised him from the dead, thou shalt be saved."* You do not have to be in a church building to confess the Lord Jesus. You can confess Him anywhere. Just confess and believe!

Recite the sinner's prayer:

> God, I am a sinner. I repent of my sins. I believe Jesus Christ died for my sins. I believe Jesus Christ rose from the dead. I accept Jesus Christ as my Lord and Savior. Dear God, please save me and make me your child.
> Amen.

Songwriter Elvina Hall wrote:

> For nothing good have I
> Whereby Thy grace to claim
> I'll wash my garment white
> In the blood of Calvary's Lamb
> Jesus paid it all
> All to Him I owe
> Sin had left a crimson stain
> He washed it white as snow[1]

Once you accept Christ as your personal Savior, go join yourself with a body of baptized believers (a church) and begin to study God's Word so the Word can become alive in you. Studying God's Word helps us to learn who He is and learn how to get closer to Him, how we should walk, and how to become a disciple (follower) of Christ.

For those who are reading and are already saved and still have feelings of being unclean, it is time to surrender all to Jesus.

Songwriter J.W. Van Deventer goes on to say:
> All to Jesus, I surrender
> Make me, Savior, wholly Thine
> Let me feel the Holy Spirit
> Truly know that Thou art mine
>
> All to Jesus, I surrender
> Lord, I give myself to Thee
> Fill me with Thy love and power
> Let Thy blessing fall on me
>
> All to Jesus, I surrender
> Now I feel the sacred flame
>
> O the joy of full salvation
> Glory, glory, to His name[2]

"If the Son therefore shall make you free [through salvation], ye shall be free indeed" (John 8:36)! Nobody can free us from whatever holds us captive like the Lord. He came to set the captives free! Be encouraged. No matter how long you have been in the closet, you can be free, and we must be free in the Lord to even stand a chance of living in a world where life is less than perfect.

**Complete workbook lesson on
"He Came to Set the Captives Free."**

9

LIFE IS LESS THAN PERFECT

"These things have I spoken unto you, that in me ye might have peace. In the world ye shall have tribulation: but be of good cheer; I have overcome the world." John 16:33

In *Becoming a Woman of Strength* by Ruth Haley Barton,[1] there is a chapter entitled "When Life is Less Than Perfect." The chapter deals with the issue of abuse, and it is centered on the story in 1 Samuel 25 about Abigail, her husband Nabal, and David (before he was King). Abigail had to deal every day with a drunken husband who was abusive. Even though Abigail may not have known God had the master plan, she knew God would intervene on her behalf when he instructed her to go to David after her husband had insulted him and his men. Nabal, her husband, had refused to offer David and his men food as a gesture of kindness after they had watched over and protected his sheep from thieves. Because God gave Abigail the strength to rise above her circumstances and the wisdom to act quickly, addressing David prevented him from killing her, her husband, and her entire household. David admired Abigail's generosity, strength, and courage to bring food and drink to him and his men. David also knew that the wisdom Abigail shared with him during their encounter could have come only from God. Abigail told

David that God would deal with her husband, and she asked David to remember her when he did. Abigail's life had been less than perfect for many years, but God stepped in. God spared Abigail and her household. Soon thereafter, Nabal died. When David heard the news of Nabal's death, he sent for Abigail and took her as his wife.

We all, through our own living, just like Abigail, can attest to the fact that life is not perfect. Here was a woman who, considered no more than property, lived daily with her husband's drunkenness and abusive behavior. Yet, instead of taking matters into her own hands, she continued to trust God, and because of her trust, He delivered her from the pit to the palace.

Perhaps Abigail was able to survive her less than perfect life because she knew, by God's revelation, there was a meaning to her life, a meaning to her suffering. Austrian psychiatrist Viktor Frankl, who survived the Holocaust, wrote in *Man's Search for Meaning,* "There is nothing in the world, I venture to say, that would so effectively help one to survive even the worst conditions as the knowledge that there is a meaning in one's life."[2]

> **"Trouble is what God uses to mold us into what He would have us to be."** Because we know we will have trouble, what is most crucial is the attitude we choose to have while we are going through our trouble.

When we look back over our lives, like Abigail, many of us could agree that it was some kind of trouble that drove us to the Lord. I once found a plaque for my mother that said: "Trouble is what God uses to mold us into what He would have us to be."

Because we know we will have trouble, what is most crucial is the attitude we choose to have while we are going through our trouble.

We do not know how Abigail's less than perfect life began, but if you were telling your story, where would you start? Having been born prematurely because my mother had fallen, my entrance into this world was a very rocky one. An unnatural and untimely separation from my mother would scar my life for a long time. The isolation in the first days of my life, I believe, precipitated that withdrawn person who later became even more withdrawn and scarred by what happened in the closet over and over again, from age four to six. My innocence had been stolen, and my childhood was wrecked. I was cast into a world of shame, silence, and secrecy. Silence became my refuge and my best friend as I lived my childhood as that invisible child. I was seen but not heard. I barely spoke unless I was spoken to. My fifth grade teacher was so concerned that she called my mother to the school for a conference. I remember her words as if it were yesterday when she asked my mother, "Does Shirley ever talk?" Momma replied, "Yes, sometimes." I surmise that since I still did my work and answered questions (even if it was only when called upon), after talking with Momma, my teacher felt no further evaluation was necessary.

Throughout junior high school, I remained a homebody and had to be forced to go outside to play. In high school, I was satisfied living in the shadows of my two older siblings. I was known as their sister. No one cared to know my name. I had no identity except to my parents. I had no boyfriends in my early teen years, even though I really had no desire for one. There was one boy I had a crush on, but he wanted more from me than I was willing to give. Sex was not an option. There was a deeply imbedded determination within me that caused me to take the position that I would never allow anyone to take anything from me ever again, especially my body. I really did not know why I felt that way, why I had to be in control of my own body, but I knew whenever I gave myself as it related to sex, it would be my choice and of my own free will. I never allowed any one to get but so close to me. I carried the weight and burden of what happened to me in that closet, never sharing it with another soul until ministry.

In young adulthood, however, the little girl who went from an invisible child to a dead woman walking began to walk in the power of the Lord's might, in the newness of a calling upon my life to preach God's Word. I finally had a voice. A voice that God said it was time to use. I had come so far, but once again, the opposite sex in my life dared to tell me to sit still, don't tell, be quiet! Hadn't I been silent long enough? The Almighty Lord was now telling me, "Talk and spread My word. Tell the world about Me, about how I can offer them freedom and how to gain eternal life." And again, man was telling me (woman) to be quiet!

Certainly, my story is not unique. How many times in history have women been looked upon as inferior, been hushed or told not to make a fuss, simply because of their gender? We who used to be the queens in our country—royalty, respected, revered, and held in high esteem—were stolen from our homes, taken from our families, and degraded to positions of enslaved "mammies," maids, bed companions for the slave master's pleasure, and milk mothers to the master's children. And told to hush—again.

If it were not for the infamous voice of a slave named Sojourner Truth, that shouted boldly at a podium at the Women's

Rights Convention in 1851, women might have been quieted forever. Regarding the notion of Black women's inferiority to White women, in particular, Truth loudly refuted, "Ain't I a woman, too?" Truth not only had to fight just to be recognized as a woman, but she also had not yet begun to address the fact that she was a Black woman who was called to preach the gospel, too.

In 1987 when God called me into the ministry, I felt like Sojourner Truth, standing in front of the Women's Rights Convention of the church world some 136 years later. I was not only saying, "Ain't I a Preacher, too," but I also wrestled with even being worthy to preach because of what happened to me in that closet—because my life was less than perfect. I wrestled with the fact that I was a woman called to preach, and women were still ostracized and considered second-class citizens, especially in the church. Why, after 136 years, were women still receiving so much resistance from the church? If we called ourselves to preach and had not been called by God, that would be one thing. The only reason people ought to seek to preach the gospel is because God called them. This calling is to serve, not to be served. It is with service in mind that one adorns the mantle of minister. Jesus said that *"whosoever will be great among you, let him be your minister; And whosoever will be chief among you, let him be your servant"* (Matthew 20:26-27). Therefore, the ministry is not a vocation whereby one seeks dominance, so men who are offended because they feel the female minister is "usurping authority over men" are erroneous in their assumption. When women who are called seek to preach, teach, or minister to anyone, they are not seeking "authority"; they are seeking to "serve," not to "rule over."

There are still some men who are not secure enough within themselves to allow women to minister unencumbered by masculine mores. There are still some churches wherein the primitive notion "women ought stay in their places" dominates. If the church is going to effectively impact society and the issues that plague both men and women, then it will have to offer more than "preaching." Such an impact will require ministry, ministry to the poor, the brokenhearted, the bruised, the blind, and the captive. Therefore, the question becomes, "Who can best minister to the women of the church, who often comprise more than 70% of local urban congregations?" Should it be men, who in most cases cannot truly identify with the painful and degrading experiences, or women? To those who so vocally declare they "don't believe in women preachers," how do women effectively "minister" to hurting women without sharing the gospel of Jesus Christ? Is such ministry not "preaching" (declaration of the Word of God) in the strictest sense of the word, even if it is a one-on-one or group counseling setting?

The hermeneutical principle of "first mention" clearly indicates that God had in mind a co-rulership of His creation when He instructed both male and female in Genesis 1:28 to *"Be fruitful and multiply, and replenish the earth, and subdue it: and have dominion."* I firmly believe the words of this verse are implicit of the fact that God holds both male and female responsible for carrying out His will on earth, as it is in heaven. Male and female are inseparable in the truest sense of the word. Will not male and female be judged equally as relates to heaven's quest of the salvation of mankind? Are not male and female equally responsible for bearing the infirmities of the weak? The salvation and well-being of the "least of these" is ascribed to male and female.

I say that anyone, male or female, who desires to sit in the pulpit for political reasons, to promote a feminist agenda, to perpetuate masculine dominance, or to raise one's self esteem, is a disgrace to the vocation. Would not it be to the adversary's benefit to keep the church mired in the male-female argument as it relates to the declaration of God's Word? Whose kingdom would benefit most from such a debate—God's kingdom or the adversary's kingdom? I believe the question of who should stand before a congregation of hurting humans should focus on *calling* rather than on *gender*.

The Serenity Prayer says, "God, grant me the Serenity to accept the things I cannot change, the Courage to change the things I can, and the Wisdom to know the difference." I believe too many people use the Serenity Prayer as an excuse to do nothing and allow wrong to sit arrogantly on the throne. This prayer is an acknowledgment of the limited nature of our human ability, hence, a call to collective prayer on behalf of the victims of any injustice. It is my conviction that a more accurate rendering of the first line of the prayer, "Lord, help me to accept the things that I cannot change," would be, "Lord, help me to accept that I cannot change certain things." I cannot

"There is nothing more right than a promise whose time has come!"

believe, and will not accept, that any injustice ought to be given automatic immunity simply because it may seem beyond the power of any human to change. All injustice, in spite of how strong or deeply rooted, must be challenged for the good of humanity and for God's namesake because He *"is no respecter of persons"* (Acts 10:34). As long as the church allows this kind of inequality to prevail, it may remain less than perfect, especially as it relates to women in ministry.

Any man who hides behind what he considers to be his interpretation of God's Word, in order to hold women back, does not know the Jesus of the Bible. Nowhere in the Bible did Jesus condone oppression of any kind in His ministry. Jesus said in Luke 4:18-19,

> *'The Spirit of the Lord is on me, because I am marked out by him to give good news to the poor; he has sent me to make well those who are broken-hearted; to say that the prisoners will be let go, and the blind will see, and to make the wounded free from their chains, To give knowledge that the year of the Lord's good pleasure is come.'* (BBE)

If the Lord chose to send His first message through a woman when He rose from the dead, what gives men the right to deny women today the opportunity to deliver His Word? A woman is not good enough to carry and deliver God's Word (from some pulpits), yet God considered a woman good enough to carry and deliver *The* Word (Jesus Christ). Therefore, be encouraged, my sisters. If you are in the ministry, do not run from place to place seeking to get ordained. Trust God. Stay and work where God has planted you. Ladies, *"Let us not be weary in well doing: for in due season we shall reap, if we faint not"* (Galatians 6:9).

I thank God that over the years, I have begun to experience the year of the Lord's good pleasure as I have witnessed a marvelous transformation on the part of many churches in their acceptance of the female minister. It is refreshing that the faithfulness and commitment of women in ministry are being recognized as genuine and effective. For too long, the people who have helped to build churches and keep them going have been barred from the pulpits of those very churches. Ironically, women who have been barred from those pulpits were barred by those who provided little support to the church until they made up their minds they were ready to commit themselves to service. However, even with such inequity, women have remained active and supportive. Through much prayer, patience, and persistence, God has stretched forth His hand and pulled back the drapery of a new day in the African American church because in the 21st century, women called to serve God in ministry are being set free in many denominations. Today, not only are women being licensed to preach the gospel in most African American churches, now women are also being ordained. The issue of women in ministry does not continue to split our denominations as much today as it did in the 20th century.

Even though life is less than perfect in some areas, we must stand so that God gets the glory. We must not go our own way but remember to *"stand firm, hold our position, and see the salvation of the Lord on your behalf"* (2 Chronicles 20:17, ESV). I can say this with conviction because sixteen years passed before I was ordained, but God kept His word to me when He said: *"There is nothing more right than a promise whose time has come."*

Little by little, the radiant light of God is illuminating the darkness and setting the captives free. No longer will God allow women to be subjected to a "nigger" status in His house. No longer is God allowing ignorance to reign like the KKK in a day when He needs all hands on deck to fight the blight of sin that pervades America. No longer is God allowing people of color to hold other people of color hostage in a place set aside for deliverance and liberation. At last, the church is looking in the mirror and seeing its own sin. At last, the grace and mercy of God are being visited upon people held in Egypt for much too long. At last, men are allowing their mothers, sisters, wives, and daughters to be free to serve God in the uniqueness of their particular calling. At last, women are free to be ministered to by the hand of someone who truly understands their feminine pain. At last, women are being blessed to feel the healing hand of a loving mother or a devoted sister. At last, a woman can feel the tender hand of another wife, who truly understands the feelings of a wife, and not feel the need to apologize for her tears. At last, a woman can feel comfortable bearing her soul without feeling as if the listener thinks she is being silly, trivial, or too sensitive. At last, the church can get ministry right, and the special qualities that only women possess can be utilized fully for the good of the kingdom. At last, and at the right time, God will *"pour out [His] spirit upon all flesh; and your sons and your daughters shall prophesy"* (Joel 2:28, emphasis added). At last!

Poet Edwin Markham said: "In all your days prepare / and meet them ever alike / when you are the anvil bear / but when you are the hammer / strike!"[3] Women, we must stay planted and be prepared. We have served our time as anvils, and many of us as hammers, but it is our time to strike! Life has not been perfect, but never let us be ashamed of who or what God made us to be because we are fearfully and wonderfully made. We are designer originals. We are the patented product of a perfect God, and after us, there was no need for God to make another thing. We are women, and this has been the case since the very beginning!

Complete workbook lesson on "Life is Less Than Perfect."

10

IN THE BEGINNING:
THE MAKING OF WOMAN

"And Adam said, This is now bone of my bone and
flesh of my flesh: she shall be called Woman, because
she was taken out of Man." Genesis 2:23

I, like so many other women, was not raised with an ever-constant reminder of how special I was. Many of us were never called "Princess" or "The apple of Daddy's eye," or told how pretty we were. Our fathers never took us on dates and showed us how to behave in the company of a young man. No one taught us what to expect and, more importantly, what to insist upon when it came men. Who told us who we were? For some of us, we were blessed to have a strong spiritual mother or father figure in our lives. For too many of us, no one told us who we were until we were born again in the body of Christ. For too many of us, the wolves disguised in sheep's clothing gave us their rendition of who we were to be and how we were to conduct ourselves.

Unless churches are exposing their young girls, teens, and women to ministry, where they can be taught who they are and whose they are, the young will grow up as most of us did—not really knowing, and the older women will never have the opportunity to know. I am a firm believer that it is never too late for women to rise from where they are to where they belong as women of God. I am a living witness because at the age of 46, this became a reality for me.

Man, in his finite mind, has tried for centuries to date the existence of God. Moses wrote in Genesis 1:1, *"In the beginning God . . ."* (emphasis added). God has existed from the beginning of time, whenever that was. The Gospel writer John further validates this fact as he writes in John 1:1, *"In the beginning was the Word, the Word was with God, and the Word was God."* God is God! God always has been and always will be. So the question remains, *what* were we, as women, intended to be from the very day of our creation? What were God's intentions for us as He fashioned us from the rib of man? The *what* of woman must be known before we can deal with the *who*, even though the two are interrelated.

THE WHAT

Imagine with me what the first woman might have given as her account:

"When God made me, Woman, W-O-M-A-N, He had out done himself. I was Woman, W-O-M-A-N, God's final crowning act of creation. I was Woman, God's glorious masterpiece. I was the pinnacle of perfection on the day I was created. In fact, I was so fine and magnificent that God had no need to create anything else! So God rested from His labor. God indeed saved the best for last!"

More than Just Body Parts

"When I was presented to Man in the garden, he was totally and undoubtedly mesmerized by my splendor! There was no one else like me in the world. Before I was called anything else, I was Woman with a capital 'W' by the one who said that

I was the epitome of him. The man to whom God gave me said: 'This is now bone of my bones and flesh of my flesh: she shall be called Woman, because she was taken out of Man' (Genesis 2:23). When Adam looked at me, a strange creature, he inspected me, and he looked hard."

Today, women are still looked at externally. If we do not pass that first inspection, like we are cattle or something, then many men do not go any further. This is sad. Our outer appearance, even though it is important, is not who we are. We cannot change what we are born with any more than a man can change what he is born with, without thousands of dollars to have plastic surgeries, implants, parts pushed up, or parts made up. It is important to note that Adam did not personalize Woman with a name until after the fall. Only after the fall does Adam refer to Woman in a personal way, when he calls her Eve. This may be theologically insignificant, but this serves to make the point that when some men first see women, they see objects, which is degrading. Man did not get personal with Woman until after the fall, but he had fallen, as well. Therefore, Adam had no right to label Woman. Adam attempted to identify and label Eve through fallen eyes just as some men continue to do today. This unfair judgment is one of the major reasons, among others, why inequality exists between men and women throughout the world to this very day.

Relationship-Oriented Being

There are two very important things we see from the first words spoken by Woman that we as women are still haunted by today. One, we always talk about how relationship-oriented women are. I believe we inherited this from the first woman. Note what Woman's first words were in Genesis 3:2, *"And the woman said unto the serpent, We may eat . . ."* The adversary in the previous verse said, "Ye," but when woman responded, she did not identify herself as an individual but a part of a union, part of her husband (Genesis 3:1). Perhaps this is why some women always identify themselves in relation to who they are married to or in relation to their children. The first woman had no idea who she was, other than the wife of Adam. She had no idea of her purpose as a woman except to be a *"help meet"* (Genesis 2:18). She did not see herself as an individual but as merely an extension of her husband.

Another important lesson that we learn from the first words of Eve, "We," is that Woman never knew what it was like to be without someone. When the first woman was created, she came into a life where everything was in place. She had a husband who had a job. She had a home, which was literally in Paradise. She had everything she would ever need. Eve was born with Adam as her covering. I believe that because the first woman was created to share her life with someone else, she never knew what it was like to be alone. Even today, many women do not like to be by themselves and sometimes, very unfortunately, will do anything just to be with someone else. Did this fact contribute to Woman's fall? I believe Woman's loneliness did indeed contribute to the fall.

Unable to handle being left alone while Adam was at "work," the woman became prey to the slippery, sinister, and sly serpent. The serpent gave Woman his undivided attention. He listened to her day after day until he was able to convince her his words were truer than the words spoken by God. Do you suppose that after a hard day's work Adam listened and gave his wife his undivided attention? Had the magic of the "Wow" worn off? Perhaps Adam had not yet developed a comfort of talking with another human being, especially someone of the opposite sex. God, in His plan, wanted to teach the couple everything they needed to know during His visits when He came down in the cool of every evening. Unfortunately, the teaching was interrupted due to sin, so man and woman caused themselves to be left floundering like fish out of water as it related to the most important tenet of any relationship—communication. Consequently, they never fully learned to communicate. This "curse" in relationships still exists today.

Sensitive Creatures

According to 1 Peter 3:7, women were created with a little more sensitivity than men, *"Likewise, ye husbands, dwell with them according to knowledge, giving honour to the wife, as unto the weaker vessel."* Peter was not talking about weaker in terms of physical strength but in terms of sensitivity. This is why in any relationship spending time getting to know one another is very important. You must spend time with an individual to learn what bothers them and what their likes and dislikes are. You must get to know them intimately (not meaning sexually) and dwell with them according to knowledge.

THE WHO

Who is this creature called Woman? Who are you, Woman? Do you think, as some men do, you are just body parts to be used and exploited and that is the total essence of your being? Do you really know who you are?

In answering this question, would a part of our answer include that we are:

Wounded

Oppressed

Misled

Angry

Negative

Although we may have these feelings, they do not have to hinder us from becoming who God created us to be. We must realize we are more than this. We are:

Wonderfully & fearfully made

Original designs

More than conquerors

Adored by God

Never alone

As it has been said before, we are in the process of becoming, and in order to become, it takes time. We do not get there overnight. The process may consist of reliving painful, unpleasant experiences of your past, but this is necessary in order to move toward wholeness. In order to get there, as uncomfortable as it may be, we must first admit that we may still have issues!

**Complete workbook lesson on
"In the Beginning: The Making of Woman."**

11

ISSUES, ISSUES, ISSUES

"A certain woman, which had an issue of blood twelve years . . .
came in the press behind, and touched his garment . . . and
straightway the fountain of her blood was dried up."
Mark 5:25-34

The story of the woman mentioned above is found in Matthew 9:20-22, Mark 5:25-34, and Luke 8:43-48. The story is told to us mainly from a physical point of view. She had an "issue" of blood for twelve long years, but I believe her "issue" was more than just physical. What was happening to and in her body was more than she knew. What was happening to this woman was more than all the doctors whose cure she sought (and to whom all her money was given) could even comprehend. The answer to her problem was not contained in their medical books or within their medical expertise. Their inability to cure this woman medically left her distressed, desperate, in despair, and still in need of healing. However, it was not until this woman sought help from Jesus for her physical issue that she received what she really needed: spiritual restoration!

In this chapter, we will discuss some of the issues that have caused, and are still causing, women to find themselves trapped in a closet. I say discuss *some* of the issues because, certainly, one book cannot address all of the issues, situations, circumstances, trials, and conditions that cause women to find themselves locked in a closet. However, we must begin somewhere. In this chapter, we will discuss the issues of abortion, abuse, anger, and absent fathers. In my years in women's ministry, these are some of the most common issues experienced by women. Some of us have never dealt with these issues. While there are others who have acknowledged they have them, but they have yet to take the necessary measures to overcome them. Sadly, there are some who do not even realize the strongholds these issues can become. Issues, issues, issues! Is one of these yours?

ABORTION

Our unborn children are being killed before they even have a chance to live! These unborn doctors, lawyers, teachers, and presidents are being murdered by various forms of abortion such as D&C,[1] saline,[2] partial birth abortion,[3] and now, the infamous morning after pill, Ru-486.[4] In September 2000, after many years of controversy, the FDA approved RU-486, the drug combination that causes abortion in early weeks of pregnancy. Feminists for Life (FFL) recommend this drug be pulled from the market immediately. The approval of RU-486 came through an accelerated drug-approval process that is usually reserved for lifesaving experimental remedies such as AIDS medications.[5] Is society implying that an "unwanted pregnancy" is a serious medical condition and a life-threatening illness?

In United States' clinical trials, which included 100 participants, despite careful screening to eliminate all but the most physically healthy candidates, 2% hemorrhaged, and several participants were hospitalized and required surgery to stop bleeding. Some participants bled for close to 60 days after taking the drug, and some developed endometriosis, an inflammation of the lining of the uterus. Worldwide, a 10% hemorrhage rate has been reported in relation to the drug, and transfusions have been required in some cases. Some of the other complications of RU-486 have been pelvic infections, resulting in sterility, nausea, vomiting, diarrhea, painful cramping, and heart palpitations. [6]

> Each year, 1.2 million pairs of little feet never learn to walk (in the United States alone), and greater than 1.2 million pairs of hands never have the opportunity to reach out and hug their mother or father. Each year, over 1.2 million little voices never get to say "Mommy" or "Daddy."

The cries of Egypt still ring out in the OB/GYN clinics and from surgical centers throughout the world as partial-birth abortion is being performed. Even though 31 states have banned this hideous act (as of 2011), partial-birth abortion remains, in my opinion, one of the most contested items in legislature.[7] Women must understand the words "partial-birth abortion." This means that the baby, which can be anywhere from four to eight months gestation, is partially delivered after the woman is dilated. The baby's feet and body are pulled out. Then, taking a sharp instrument, the baby's skull is punctured and removed by sucking out the brains or by crushing the skull. Then, the baby is removed from the mother's body.

Each year, 1.2 million pairs of little feet never learn to walk (in the United States alone), and greater than 1.2 million pairs of hands never have the opportunity to reach out and hug their mother or father. Each year, over 1.2 million little voices never get to say "Mommy" or "Daddy."[8]

I know this may sound harsh or even dredge up painful memories, but I do not want you to live in the guilt and shame of your past any longer! God has forgiven you if you have asked Him for forgiveness. I beg anyone who may be contemplating abortion because of fear of what others may think, fear of raising the child alone, or fear of the embarrassment of how the child was conceived, please do not do it! I beg you to reconsider because the cries of our babies are ringing out. They have no chance but the chance we give them. They have no voice but our voices to speak out for their lives. Jesus said, *"I am come that they might have life, and that they might have it more abundantly"* (John 10:10).

In 2003, on the 30th anniversary of Roe v. Wade, there was an advertisement in *The Washington Post* that said: "Women Deserve Better." When my pastor showed me this ad, he asked me what I thought this quote meant. Immediately, I thought about the mental and spiritual anguish some women suffer who have had an abortion. One may say this only applies to non-Christians. My response: I adamantly disagree. Though Christians know about the forgiving grace of Christ, from my observations in ministry, I have found that, too often, women cannot forgive themselves. It is not until they allow themselves to become open to the freeness of forgiveness that they can receive and walk in the forgiveness that only Christ can provide. Without that freedom, they may continue to suffer a thousand deaths, over and over again, in their minds, bodies, and spirits.

I know that reading this may have recalled some horrible memories or feelings of guilt or shame. If you have already asked God to forgive you, walk in His forgiveness! If you have not asked for His forgiveness, take a moment to do it now.

> Father, You have assured me that I can cast all my cares upon You because You care for me. So, I come now, in the name of Jesus, confessing that I have sinned. I had an abortion and terminated a life. Please forgive me and help me to forgive myself. Today, I receive the peace that I have so long sought. Thank You.
> *In Jesus' name, Amen.*

Remember that God will forgive us for anything, *anything*, that we have done (except blasphemy against the Holy Ghost). If you are still suffering from the effects of abortion, seek spiritual counseling, then professional counseling, if needed. I have repeated it many times in this book: We must be moving toward healing from our past in order to enjoy the present (which is a gift from God), or there will not be much of a future.

ABUSE

With me, life went well for many years until, one day, my world began to crumble little by little when I came face to face with my closet captor in a ministry class. A horrifying fear arose in me like none I had ever experienced, except when the nightmares tried to escape from my subconscious to my conscious mind. Suppression plays a major role in the life of someone who has been sexually abused. It is a mechanism used to block out the tragic experience so one may cope with life. Denial is also prevalent. The extent of the denial is what is deadly, according to Kathleen, author of *Healing from Sexual Abuse*[9]. In Kathleen's book, she shares her own story and explains to readers that when victims deny the past, they are forced to spend an enormous amount of psychological energy burying the pain. I agree with Kathleen's assertion that no one can deny and suppress pain without personal damage. She explains that deep pain does not just go away, nor can it be wished away. Instead, one must talk it through, pray it through, and sometimes, even cry it through.[10]

As survivors of abuse, we must recognize that we are not responsible for what was done to us. One question that is always foremost in the mind of a person who has been abused is, *"Will the pain ever go away?"* The pain of remembering seems unbearable sometimes. In that class session where my closet captor presented himself is when I first faced the fact that the "nightmare" about the molestation was not a "nightmare," it was real. This is when I began to face the reality of what happened and began the process of healing. Unfortunately, for

> **One question that is always foremost in the mind of the person who has been abused is, *"Will the pain ever go away?"***

some women, the reality of a closet experience is too difficult to confront. Someone in the same class briefly confessed the abuse she experienced but could no longer talk about it and stopped coming to the sessions. She was referred to outside counseling so she could continue to work through that stronghold at her own pace, under much-needed supervision and guidance.

As stated earlier in chapter seven ("Who Am I?"), what happens to us in the creational phase of our development, as described by Cynthia Hicks, can influence the type of relationships in which we involve ourselves. Sadly, this sometimes includes our involvement with males who have abusive tendencies, males who, more than likely, have been abused themselves. Unfortunately, being in these types of relationships can often lead to death of the victim, the abuser, or both.

For example, in January 2000, a young woman named Janice Lancaster[11] lost her life tragically. Due to a court's negligence, Lancaster's estranged husband was not taken into custody for charges of physical abuse and stalking. Shortly after being released from court, Janice Lancaster was murdered by her husband. After he took her life, he took his, as well. Their two children discovered their bodies.

In order to be healed from any form of abuse, victims must deal with the "crime of secrecy." The crime of secrecy refers to experiencing any form of abuse and not telling. Abuse is about power and control. The pain of what was done in no way compares to the pain of keeping silent about what was done. By keeping silent, we give the abuse and the abuser the power to keep us enslaved and in darkness. As difficult as it may be, the only way for us to begin to move toward the light is to take away their power by revealing what happened. As Geri Redden, the founder and executive director of the National Center for Violence Prevention (NCVP),[12] explains, "When it [the secret] is out in the light, it cannot live anymore." We must admit the abuse and begin the process of healing.

Healing comes from recognizing you were wronged—that someone else violated you, that it was not your fault, and that forgiveness of the violator(s) is imperative—but forgiveness and healing do not have to involve confronting others or even naming one's abuser. However, if you feel this is what you need to do (confronting and naming) to achieve wholeness, then you will have to venture on that journey seeking wisdom, guidance, and direction from God.

ANGER

"Holding on to anger is like grasping a hot coal with the intent to throw it at someone else; [but] you are the one that gets burned."[13] Gautama Siddharta

As I grew into my teen years, I was determined I would never again allow anyone to touch me in an inappropriate manner. I would be in control. Perhaps the most profound effect of what happened to me, aside from only talking when I was spoken to, was anger. I was, and still am to a certain extent, angry! Angry because I was told to be quiet. Angry because I felt all alone. Angry because this should not have happened to me. As an adult, I am angry because the world, the workplace, and especially some places of worship today, are seen as a "man's domain." Angry because, even in this 21st century, the "good ole boy" system is still dominant. Angry because even in the church, a place where women outnumber men, sometimes six to one, men seem to reign. Angry because so-called biblical scholars can theorize and exegete the Word of God, while the will of God is being supplanted by the insensitive whim of men, men who steal the dignity and rights of women in the house of God. Men who refuse to acknow- ledge that women have ever been mistreated. Men who seek to minimize our pain. Men

> In many churches, wounded and abused women must receive ministry from people who are insensitive to their plight and who feel threatened by their recovery.

who sometimes even smirk when the subjects of chauvinism and discrimination are raised. Men who exacerbate our frustration by utilizing sarcasm and patronizing words. Men who wound us further, even from the pulpit. I continue to be angry because Sunday after Sunday women come to the church hurting, bleeding profusely from abuse and discrimination. Angry because the one place that is supposed to be a sanctuary for people hurt and hounded by the demonic forces of this world is often the same place where the wounded are shot and salt poured into their open wounds. The lonely often are pushed further into alienation and isolation. I still get angry because, in many churches, wounded and abused women must receive ministry from people who are insensitive to their plight and who feel threatened by their recovery.

Yes, I must admit that African American men who are old enough to know what it feels like to be discriminated against, merely because of the circumstances of their birth, often anger me. Such men unknowingly (or knowingly) perpetuate the humiliation and degradation of what happened to me, and millions of women just like me who come through the doors of churches across America every Sunday morning (doors, by the way, that we women have mostly paid for). This treatment from men adds to the never-ending pain and feelings of being raped, molested, beaten, and taken advantage of over and over again. This type of treatment promotes death—not life.

Although I still become angry about some of these things, ministry has helped me with the healing of these wounds and has also helped me begin the process of releasing this anger before it hardens into bitterness or explodes into rage. As a ministry leader, God has afforded me the opportunity to help countless other women deal with the anger that originated in a closet or in a church. This type of anger, if left untreated, can become self-destructive and detrimental to our relationships with the opposite sex.

I never knew I was suffering from anger as a result of my innocence being stolen until I began to face the darkness of my past. I truly had to embrace the fact that it was possible to display the calmness of still waters on the outside yet feel like a raging volcano on the inside. To me, society has always perpetuated the notion that men had cornered the market as it relates to anger. However, having been involved with women's ministry for nearly two decades, I can attest that women, too, suffer from anger issues.

Gary Oliver and H. Norman Wright suggest that one must identify and understand the root cause of one's anger. They contend that, generally, when women deal with anger, there is not just one reason they are angry. Emotions stemming from fear, hurt, frustration, double standards, injustice, gender bias, unrewarded work, and shame may be root causes that have led to feelings of anger. Oliver and Wright note, "Society's seeming openness to women's issues is calling forth emotions that Christian women have eschewed for centuries."[14] I strongly believe that because many women have not dealt with this issue of anger, the need for women's ministry has reached monumental proportion.

There are many reasons why women experience so much anger from childhood to adulthood, but one of the major contributors to our anger (and I would venture to say the anger of men, as well) is the absence of fathers.

ABSENT FATHER

In this chapter, I am defining absent fathers as:

☦ Fathers who are physically not there and/or

☦ Fathers who are physically there, but who are so emotionally unattached they are either unaware of what their daughters are going through, too overwhelmed with their own issues to deal with their daughters' issues, or worse yet, simply unwilling to care

Imagine having to deal with the aforementioned topics of abortion, abuse, and anger in addition to an "absentee father." The absentee father not only affects the child and the family unit but also affects the entire country as a whole. One study, focusing on the annual public costs of father absence, the first of its kind, provides an estimate of the taxpayer costs of the absence of fathers. It estimates the annual expenditures made by the federal government to support father-absent homes. In 2006, the study reports the federal government spent at least 99.8 billion dollars assisting father-absent families.[15] The study also reports that father absence has risen greatly in the last four decades. Between 1960 and 2006, the number of children living in single-mother families went from 8 percent to 23.3 percent, and 34 percent of children currently live absent from their biological father.

Other statistics in reference to the effects of father absence are staggering. For example, father absence contributes to family poverty and infant mortality.[16] It also contributes to higher incidences of teen pregnancies.[17] In a study of 13,986 women in prison, more than half of them grew up in a father-absent home.[18] Additionally, children in father-absent homes are at greater risk of being physically and sexually abused.[19]

The four-fold, catastrophic calamity of abortion, abuse, anger and the absentee father has created almost insurmountable strongholds in the lives of many women. First, we must admit we have issues, and then, we must learn how to deal with them in order to loosen the grip these strongholds have had, are having, and will have in the future. One thing I always want you to remember is, regardless of what name the issue may have, certainly, there is nothing too hard for God. Ladies, stand strong, look the issue directly in the face, and boldly proclaim: *"For this, I have Jesus!"*

In an effort to rid our lives of the crippling effects of these issues, we must take action. The process begins by throwing away the garbage we have collected and allowed to pile up in the core of our very being.

Complete workbook lesson on "Issues, Issues, Issues."

12

Take out the Trash & Throw away the Garbage

"Lay aside every weight, and the sin which doth so easily beset us, and let us run with patience the race that is set before us, Looking to Jesus the author and finisher of our faith" Hebrews 12:1b-2a

We discussed in previous chapters some of the issues that cause us to become closet captives. We now know there is a need for ministry in order to come into the knowledge of who we are and whose we are. Through ministry, we discover that Jesus came to set the captives free, even though life is less than perfect, and it has been this way since the beginning (of sin). Now, it is time to take out the trash and throw away the garbage. In this chapter, we will discuss what we need to do in order to come out of the closets we are already in, and we will also learn what preventive measures we can take to stay out of closets in the future. There are many issues that can lead us into the closet, some finding root in our childhood like the issues I experienced. However, no matter the problem that put us in the closet and no matter how long we may have been in the closet, Jesus is the closet opener!

The sin and weight addressed in Hebrews chapter 12 can be equated to trash and garbage. Both must be discarded and must be disposed of in a certain way so others do not become ill. Trash and garbage must be disposed of because they are not healthy for the person in possession of them or for the people who might be exposed to them. Traditionally, taking out the trash and throwing away the garbage has not been the woman's job. In our spiritual walk, however, if we want to live the abundant life that Jesus promised us, after accepting Christ as our personal Savior, we must begin the process of dumping the baggage owned by the old man (old sin nature).

We must do our part and take the trash and garbage to the curb. In days of old, you could not mix trash and garbage because they were not the same. There was trash, which was dry and could invite insects, and garbage, which was leftover food and had the potential to grow parasites and attract rodents. You had to put them into separate containers. Then and now, no one will come into our house to get our trash and our garbage. The system does not work that way. Spiritually, Jesus waits with great anticipation for us to bring Him our burdens. He not only wants us to bring our burdens to Him, but He encourages us to do so. He said in Matthew 11:28: *"Come unto me, all ye that labour and are heavy laden, and I will give you rest."* Throughout the book of Psalms, David identifies the Lord as our burden bearer, our heart fixer, and our mind regulator. We can take our burdens to the Lord and leave them there. Actually, songwriter Charles Albert Tindley[1] says in "Leave It There" to "Take your burden [singular] to the Lord and leave *it* there" (emphasis mine). I believe Tindley makes a point to tell us to leave *it* there (singular) is in hopes that if we ever get it right, just once without hesitation or reservation, we would take our burden each time and leave it there. People don't take out their trash and garbage and drag them back into the house. Even if we forgot it is a holiday or put the trash or garbage out too late, we would leave it outside, tightly sealed, until the next collection day. Why do we continue to take our burdens to the Lord and insist on picking them up and carrying them back?

Usually, more so than men, women become very adept at physically collecting items we do not need. Sometimes, we even collect and store items that belong to other people, which make our load even heavier. In the same manner, year after year, we often mentally and emotionally collect issues from others to add to the trunk of issues from our past that we have never dealt with—to our own detriment.

The type of receptacle we choose to collect and store these items and issues in usually progresses from a bag to a suitcase to a trunk.

BAG LADY

A growing problem of today is "bag women." We can see them in cities all across America. What they carry in the bag limits them and weighs them down. If they develop real trust in Christ, they can leave not only what is *in the bags* but also leave the bags themselves because "one day all them bags gone get in your way, so . . . / Let it go, let it go, let it go, let it go."[2]

LUGGAGE HANDLER

Because we have not learned how to deal with our issues that are in the bag, we continue to collect items. Then, we need a larger storage space—a suitcase. Suitcases can be very deceiving, not because they come in so many sizes but because we no longer have to physically carry them by the handle. We can comfortably roll around our issues from place to place—and we think we are doing something! Initially, suitcases can appear to be convenient, allowing you to pack and transport easily your items and issues from one place to another. However, as we continue to pack and carry without ever emptying, our suitcases become too weighted down, the handles break, and then the wheels fall off. This forces us to have to physically (or in some cases, mentally) carry these items, unpack them, or look for a larger storage container.

I used to say that women come to the altar Sunday after Sunday dragging or rolling the same suitcase back and forth. Well, today, we have moved beyond the suitcase to those really big footlockers. You know, those big trunks that allow us to organize our mess.

TRUNK TOTER

Trunks usually have many compartments. Let's look at the TRUNK and examine the contents of each compartment:

T – TALK (Proverbs 18:21, MSG)
"Words kill, words give life; they're either poison or fruit–you choose."

All of those negative things that people have said to us or about us; the words that have scarred us deeply; the sticks and stones that may not have necessarily broken our bones, but the words (the negative talk) that have certainly damaged our spirits, broken our hearts, scarred our self-esteem, and threatened to destroy us.

R – REJECTION (Psalm 34:18, NIV)
"The Lord is close to the brokenhearted and saves those who are crushed in spirit."

Whether the rejection began as a little girl, a budding teen, or a young woman, it may haunt us in every relationship for the rest of our lives. If we do not deal with it, it will deal with us.

U – UNFORGIVENESS (Matthew 6:14-15, NKJV)
"For if you forgive men their trespasses, your heavenly Father will also forgive you. But if you do not forgive men their trespasses, neither will your Father forgive your trespasses."

This compartment is running over with lots of issues, as you will see in the chapter "Forgiveness." Unless we begin to unpack this compartment, we will never truly be free.

N – NEGATIVE SELF-ESTEEM (Psalm 139:14, CEV) *"And I praise you because of the wonderful way you created me. Everything you do is marvelous! Of this I have no doubt.*

Our self-esteem develops from the early years of our lives. It is impacted by our upbringing and by both our positive and negative experiences. Our greatest hope for positive self-esteem comes from our relationship with God as our Creator.

K – KNOWLEDGE DEFICIT (Hosea 4:6, KJV) *"My people are destroyed for lack of knowledge."*

In order to unpack our TRUN, we must conqueror the "K." It is through the "K" that we discover what we do not KNOW. It is through the "K" that we learn, for the first time in most of our lives, who we are and whose we are. We can only know this through a personal relationship with God. It is through our knowledge of God and His Word that we move from being bound, broken, and bent to wonderfully made, wise, and whole (Hosea 4:6).

In order for us to move toward healing, we must deal with the trash and garbage we are still carrying around from our past. Whether our issues are housed in bags or suitcases or packed neatly away in the trunks of our minds, we must deal with them. We must deal with these issues and let the perfect love of Christ heal us of our issues. Many of us have never dealt with the molestation, the rape, the physical and mental abuse, the drugs, the prostitution, the adultery, the divorce, the abandonment, the rejection, or the guilt of having an abortion.

Think about this in the natural sense. We know what happens to garbage when it stays around too long. It begins to stink and maggots will take up residence in it. The bacteria that grow in the garbage and trash begin to give off toxic, offensive odors. Eventually, the possessor becomes sick from the foamy, frothy foulness that is contained within. What is even more critical here is that not only does the possessor of the trash and garbage become deathly ill if they do not dispose of the contents, but also anyone living with them can become sick or infected by what they are carrying. Anyone who gets close to them will smell the stench and avoid them.

When we continue to walk around holding on to all the garbage of our past, not only do maggots take up residence, but we also give off a stench in God's nostrils. Trash that stays around too long will begin to attract flies, roaches, rats, and anything else that can crawl in the bags and hide. These maggots, insects, and rodents can represent guilt, depression, shame, bitterness, or unforgiveness, just to name a few. They also may represent unhealthy relationships with other people who are also carrying around garbage.

When we get sick physically, emotionally, and spiritually, we may spend many countless hours trying to figure out why. Sometimes, we are fully aware of what is weighing us down and just think time will take care of it. *If I ignore whatever it is that grips my very soul and sickens me, I can close my eyes and pretend it never happened. When I open my eyes, it will just go away, and I will be okay.* I can tell you with certainty that it will never just go away. The trash and garbage from our past will continue to weigh us down, hold us captive, and push people away from us, thereby keeping us as dead women walking. Unless we get rid of such weight, we will never live—we will only exist. When we really get sick and tired of being sick and tired because of

> We must evict them!
> Throw them out!
> Then pad lock the
> door and put up a
> "No Vacancy" sign!

all the *stuff* we are carrying, then we will meet the conditions to receive healing—and Jesus will step in. My pastor often quotes a Buddhist proverb, "When the student is ready, the teacher will appear." Are you ready yet?

As the title of this chapter implies, we must take some action. We cannot simply take these weights, whatever name they may have, and gently set them out on the curbs of our lives. No, we must evict them! Throw them out! Then padlock the door and put up a "No Vacancy" sign! The adversary will never willingly go away. He must be driven away! He must be cast out by the power found in God's Word, by the power resonating in the name of Jesus, and by the power of prayer. Cleaning out those hidden cobwebs, sweeping the trash from under the porch, taking out the garbage, and getting rid of the rats, roaches, flies, and the foamy, frothy, foul-smelling, maggot-infested contents we carry within frees up space inside so the Holy Spirit can come in and reside. This strengthens our relationships, helps us become more focused on our purpose for existing, and helps us become the instruments, the women, that God would be proud to use anytime and anywhere. We must face the truth about ourselves as John 8:32 says: *"And ye shall know the truth, and the truth shall make you free."*

In my experience in ministering to women, it is exhilarating to hear them say that for the first time in 10, 20, 30, or more than 40 years, they are free. They know they are forgiven for having children out of wedlock, for having an abortion, for having committed adultery, for prostitution, or for addictions of any kind. Through ministry, women learn they do not have to allow themselves to be abused physically, emotionally, or economically in order to feel loved. We must know without any doubt that God cares for us. God loves us unconditionally! It is not about what we have done. It is not about what was done to us, but it is about what Jesus did for us, is doing for us, and will continue to do for us. He paid the price for all of our sins, sorrows, sicknesses, struggles, heartaches, humiliations, hurts, disappointments, depressions, and discouragements. Jesus paid it all on Calvary. Jesus said: *"The thief cometh not, but for to steal, and to kill, and to destroy: I am come that they might have life, and that they might have it more abundantly"* (John 10:10). The question is, "Do you want abundant life, and if you do, how badly do you want it?"

If we as women are determined to be free, then we must constantly examine ourselves, looking deeply within and facing the truth about ourselves. We must look at what is weighing us down. When we reflect on our lives, past and present, what or who would we say is holding us captive? What or who is keeping us from growing emotionally, financially, and most importantly, spiritually? We do an assignment in the ministry called: "What's in the Bag?" The "bag" is symbolic of our life. Whatever we are burdened with, we carry from place to place—from one day to another, from one week to another, from one month to another, and yes, even from one year to another—until we are delivered or we die, whichever comes first.

I do not believe it is anyone's desire to stay burdened with the cares of this world. As children of God, we must know that Jesus came to set the captives free. We may have been under the impression that Jesus was simply talking about being captive to sin and only talking about salvation. However, His mission

> Even children of God have the potential to and are more likely to be held captive by some situation, circumstance, or even people, if we permit them to hold us prisoner.

encompassed much more than that. We also may have thought that once we are saved from the penalty of sin, we are no longer captive to the power of sin! Well, I do not mean to shatter your belief, but you need to understand that even children of God have the potential to (and are more likely to) be held captive by some situation, circumstance, or even people, if we permit them to hold us prisoner.

When we are struggling with the issues of life, we must know that God permits some issues so that He may be glorified, as found in John 9:3 in the case of the young man born blind from birth. The disciples asked Jesus who sinned, the man or his parents. Jesus said neither, *"but that the works of God should be made manifest in him."* In other words, this man's healing was ordained to be at the specific time in which it occurred. God, being all-wise, knowing where the man would be at that time, knowing where Jesus would be at that time, healed the man at that very moment so He would be glorified in the eyes and hearts of the people who witnessed the miraculous event.

Do we honestly think the only people who are in prison are those locked behind the prison walls? No, many of us—saved, sanctified, Holy Ghost filled, fire baptized, children of the most High King—are in bondage! The question we need to ask ourselves today is what or who has us in bondage.

The workbook lesson associated with this chapter will give us a process we can follow in any situation that creates bondage or strongholds in our lives. This process prompts you to take action, and that is precisely what we need to do. Freedom requires

> Many of us—saved, sanctified, Holy Ghost filled, fire baptized, children of the most High King—are in bondage!

ACTS to become loosed. We must Acknowledge, Confess, Trust, and Step Out.

The first step to freedom is to *Acknowledge* there is a problem(s). For years, as you have read, I never dealt with what was in my bag. I pretended it was just a bad dream. I pretended it was a nightmare, and when I awakened from my sleep, everything would be all right. From the age of 4 until 42, I remained trapped as the little girl in the closet and grew up to become a dead woman walking.

Half of the battle has been won when we acknowledge or admit there is a problem. Sometimes, the problem may not be a what, but a who. Sometimes, it may be a combination of the two. We have become very adept at smiling and hiding behind the many masks we wear from day to day. We may even feel that if we pray hard enough, the issue will go away. Not necessarily so. The problem must be acknowledged. It was being involved in ministry that helped me realize this.

The second step to freedom is to *Confess the problem(s)*. Even with the writing of this book, it took me 33 years to confess to my husband what happened to me as a child. The silence that I found refuge in for so many years as the invisible child, and the vivid memory of the words whispered in my ear in that closet never to tell, kept me in bondage. You may be thinking over and over in your mind, just as I did, trying to find the right words, trying to find the right time to confess. The time will come. It must come in order to move toward healing and wholeness. I pray it has not been as long for you as it was for me, but if it has, today can be the first day of the rest of your life.

Confess to the Lord, first. Tell Him what He already knows. Then, as ministry to yourself (or if participating in a group session), confess those things in writing. List those things you have acknowledged as problems. There may come a time when you can talk about those closet issues openly, but until then, confess them by writing them down.

Confessing requires us to STRIP, **S**top to **R**eveal **I**nternal **P**roblems. We must become naked and not ashamed before the Lord. We must tell the Lord what He already knows and pour out, empty out, and strip off everything that weighs us down. We must become lighter by losing some weight. Not weight in terms of being physically heavy, but weight as it relates to what is in our bags. Stripping before the Lord is a process, and it does not happen overnight. This is why women's ministry is so important. All of the weight and burdens we have been carrying around for 5, 10, 20, 30, or 40 years or more can be discarded by beginning to

STRIP. The environment in which we begin to STRIP, however, is very crucial. Ministry is one of the best environments to begin this process. As we STRIP, we will begin to discover who we are and what our true purpose is in order to have abundant life.

When there are wounds, generally, there are SCARS, and in order for us to move toward healing and wholeness, we must be willing to show our SCARS.

Suffering	Sickness
Condemnation	Curses
Abandonment	Abuse
Rejection	Ridicule
Sorrows	Struggle

We must expose our scars, in addition to stripping off those things or people holding us captive, in order for the freedom process truly to be completed. I once heard someone say that if we survived yesterday, there is a very strong possibility we will survive today and a great hope we can make it through tomorrow.

The third step in the process to freedom is *Trust God and His Word*. Holding on to God and His Word kept me. My relationship with the Lord kept me sane. The preached Word, the written Word, and the sang Word kept me encouraged. I held on and refused to let go. Proverbs 3:5-6 teaches us to trust God for who He is, and if we do that, He will guide us in every area of our lives: "*Trust in the Lord with all thine heart; and lean not unto thine own understanding. In all thy ways acknowledge him; and he shall direct thy path*" (emphasis mine). Understand that fully trusting the Lord with all our hearts in every situation is a process, an ongoing process. Pastor McCoy recently introduced to us a life-altering quote, "Everything will bow to God this day!" There is nothing that can happen in which God is excluded, unaware of, or not asked permission when it comes to His children, nor will anything happen that God cannot handle on our behalf!

To trust God is also to trust His Word. There are over 7,400 promises in God's Word, and I assure you He spoke one of them just for you and what you are dealing with. Begin to search God's Word by subject matter. Get a good topical reference book for the Bible, and list those passages of scripture that apply to what is holding you captive. Jesus says in Matthew 22:29a, *"Ye do err, not knowing the scriptures."* As we search the scriptures, we should write out those passages one by one. Write them on index cards. Put them on your mirror, on your refrigerator, on your desk at work, or any other place you can look at them often.

> How do you help someone through his or her pain or hurt when that same someone is contributing to the pain and hurt in your life?

Once you have found God's promise:

Repeat the promise over and over again
Meditate on the promise until you
Believe it for yourself
Speak the promise to your situation
Pray the promise

The adversary cares nothing about our words, what we think, or how we feel. When we pray, we need to tell him what our God has promised us in His Word and let him know that if God said it, that settles it!

We must PUSH (**P**ray **U**ntil **S**omething **H**appens) because prayer changes things. We must PRAY because **P**rayer **U**pholds,

Sustains, and Heals. When we PRAY often, **P**roblems **R**arely **A**ffect **Y**ou and **P**ower will **R**eign **A**ll **Y**ear.

The fourth step in the process to freedom is to ***Step*** *out on faith.* Acknowledging the problem, confessing it, and trusting God and His Word may end up being the easy steps in this process called freedom. Once the problem is acknowledged and confessed (whether openly or in writing), we must trust God and His Word as we live with the decision to be free. At this point, as we begin to step out on faith, it is almost a certainty that we will still battle with feelings of guilt or shame and have thoughts that people are whispering about what we have just revealed. Even in our social vulnerability, if we continue to trust God and His promises, we will discover that the GRIP (**G**rueling, **R**elentless, and **I**nward **P**ain) of whatever happened will begin to abate.

We must not become discouraged as we begin this process. Changes do not happen overnight, and we must not judge ourselves based on what we see or do not see. William Newton Clarke once noted, "Faith is the daring of the soul to go farther than it can see,"[3] and the apostle Paul says in II Corinthians 5:7, *"For we walk by faith, not by sight."* We must stand with our heads held high. As children of God, we are *"a chosen generation, a royal priesthood"* (1 Peter 2:9), more precious than gold. When stepping out on faith, we must:

> *Begin* to thank Him for answering our prayers
> *Begin* to walk in victory
> *Begin* to talk positively (speaking life, instead of death, into our situation – Proverbs 18:21)
> *Begin* to live in victory!

In order to move forward, we must stop living in the past: *"Forgetting those things which are behind, and reaching forth unto those things which are before, I press toward the mark for the prize of the high calling of God in Christ Jesus"* (Philippians 3:13-14).

How do you help someone through his or her pain and hurt when that same someone is contributing to the pain and hurt in your life? We cannot within ourselves (nor do we even want to), but through Christ, we can. For it is not by our strength or our power, but by His. Zechariah 4:6b says, *"Not by might, nor by power, but by my spirit, saith the Lord of hosts."* Christ looked beyond His excruciating pain on the cross and saw His perpetrators' need for forgiveness, and He prayed for them. His prayer was so effective until a Roman centurion solider (a heathen) declared that surely this must be the Son of God. Therefore, as children of God, we also can pray for those who are inflicting pain upon us.

I was inspired by a passage I read in the November 14, 2005 *Daily Bread*. The passage cited English novelist Aldous Huxley, "There are no back moves on the chessboard of life." With this in mind, we should rejoice! God has *"cast all [our] sins into the depths of the sea"* (Micah 7:19). Are you still concerned about your sins? Rejoice! *"Their sins and iniquities will I remember no more"* (Hebrews 10:17). *"I have blotted out, as a thick cloud, thy transgressions,"* says the Lord (Isaiah 44:22).

If you have put your faith in Jesus and asked God to forgive you, the past truly is forgotten: *"As far as the east is from the west, so far hath he removed our transgressions from us"* (Psalm 103:12). Trust and rejoice! It is time to accept forgiveness and begin to forgive others.

**Complete workbook lesson on
"Take out the Trash & Throw away the Garbage."**

13

FORGIVENESS

"If we confess our sins, he is faithful and just to forgive us our sins, and to cleanse us from all unrighteousness." 1 John 1:9

"But if ye do not forgive [others' trespasses], neither will your Father which is in heaven forgive your trespasses." Mark 11:26

FORGIVING OTHERS

"If it were not for God's forgiving grace, heaven would be empty." – German proverb

"Put on therefore, as the elect of God, holy and beloved, bowels of mercies, kindness, humbleness of mind, meekness, longsuffering; Forbearing one another, and forgiving one another, if any man have a quarrel against any: even as Christ forgave you, so also do ye." Colossians 3:12–13

I contemplated addressing this topic in a previous chapter, but this subject is so essential to healing and wholeness (as well as one of the major areas of bondage) that it warranted a section of its own. Unforgiveness is a debilitating and destructive prison. It destroys the person who refuses to forgive and often can destroy the one who is not forgiven. I teach the women in the ministry that forgiveness = freedom. Forgiving is a choice! As children of God, we may say it is not a choice but a mandate to forgive. Well, that statement may be half-right and half-wrong, if there is such a thing. God made us with a free will to choose, so we have free will to choose whether to forgive or not. Nevertheless, God makes it very clear in His Word what the consequences will be if we choose not to forgive (Mark 11:26). Nancy DeMoss states in her book *Choosing Forgiveness: Your Journey to Freedom*,[1] "We cannot expect to live at peace with God or to experience His blessing in our lives if we refuse to forgive our debtors." She goes on to say, "The wounds that have been inflicted upon [us] will not be made one ounce lighter by being stored up and left to fester. In fact, they will only become heavier and more burdensome."

When we judge, punish, and sentence people to a life of hell on earth because they have messed up, I am sure this makes God wonder when He established a *fourth* part of the Trinity and how *we* became qualified to take the job. How dare we forsake and abandon those we claim to love because they did not dot every "I" and cross every "T" or respond the way we thought they should have? I am not talking about allowing people to totally run over and abuse us. I am talking about people making a mistake, and then we make them suffer a lifetime for it.

Have you ever found yourself angry with someone because they did not do something the way you thought they should have done it? Have you ever found yourself angry because what someone did reflected negatively on you, so you rejected that person? Our initial response is usually, *"How could they have done that to me? Who do they think they are?"* What right do we have to hold people to standards that we cannot meet? Paul warns us about thinking more highly of ourselves than we ought. Do we feel we are so perfect that we can never disappoint others, even unintentionally?

If we feel we never do anything to disappoint others, *"if we say that we have no sin, we deceive ourselves, and the truth is not in us"* (I John 1:8)! If we as humans are not above reproach, then what makes us feel we are never to experience disappointment? Is it because we feel we treat others so well that we should not have to experience the sting of disappointment? If we feel this way, then we place ourselves above God. Did not Jesus experience disappointment and rejection when He was here from His kindred, from those He fed and healed, and from those with whom He walked? I often wonder where we would be today if God dealt with our mistakes and sins in the same manner—with unforgiveness.

THINK ABOUT THIS . . .

✞ Never asking for forgiveness as well as never forgiving is to be as a dead person.

✞ Never asking for forgiveness or never forgiving is to live in a spiritual hell.

✞ Never asking for forgiveness or never forgiving is to live in an emotional hell.

✞ Never asking for forgiveness or never forgiving means you can never know true freedom or true peace.

✝ Never asking for forgiveness or never forgiving is to say, *"I never want the forgiveness of God."* Mark 11:26 says: *"But if ye do not forgive, neither will your Father which is in heaven forgive your trespasses."*

To mistreat someone, especially those of the household of faith, is synonymous with mistreating God. Stormie Omartian, in her book *The Power of a Praying Woman*,[2] talks about layers of unforgiveness that we can have for just one person. Omartian does not list any specific layers, but I propose that what those layers would be are different for each of us based on our experiences. The main point that Omartian emphasizes, however, is that forgiveness is a choice! She encourages readers to think about who they need to forgive and who they need to ask for forgiveness. I would also say we need to think about: *"Is the person you need to forgive yourself or someone else? What do you need to forgive them or yourself for? How has what they have done to you affected your life? How has what you have done affected your life? What have been the short- and long-term effects?"*

Unforgiveness is a form of pride. When someone has wronged us, we have a natural desire to see justice done. When we withhold forgiveness, we are passing judgment on the person. God instructs us to trust in Him for the execution of justice. Scripture says, *"Beloved, do not avenge yourselves, but rather give place to wrath; for it is written, 'Vengeance is Mine, I will repay,' says the Lord"* (Romans 12:19, NKJV). We must submit our desire for justice to Him and trust it in His hands.

Bitterness, anger, and malice toward a person always raise their ugly heads. Our unforgiving spirit is often evident in how we view the object of our bitterness, anger, or malice. The ugliness of this trio is often heard in the numerous hurtful, sarcastic remarks we make directly to the object of our anger, but then we try to play it off with: "I was just kidding." Additionally, we make these unnecessary remarks within earshot of the person to ensure they hear us. When the person asks us about our remarks, we say: "Oh, I wasn't talking about you." We need to stop lying! In most cases, we say these hurtful things because we want to make the person feel like we feel when they hurt us. It's called payback! It's called, "That's okay; I'll get you. Vengeance is mine!"

Have you ever held bitterness in your heart for years? Have you ever said to yourself you would never forgive someone for what he or she did to you? Have you ever said to someone else: *"I'll never forgive so and so for what they did?"* Have you ever said to someone: *"I'll never forgive you for what you did to me?"*

Have you ever held bitterness in your heart because the person who wronged you never apologized or never even acknowledged what they did to you? You may never receive an apology of any kind but that is okay, *"But let judgment run down as waters, and righteousness as a mighty stream"* (Amos 5:24). Just remember, the only way for us to be free is to forgive others. And sometimes, with the awesome charge of forgiving others for what they have done, we experience the awesome weight of having to forgive ourselves for what we have done.

FORGIVING SELF

"Come now, and let us reason together, saith the Lord: though your sins be as scarlet, they shall be white as snow; though they be red like crimson, they shall be as wool." Isaiah 1:18

We never remember how many times we have personally disappointed God, those times when we failed to do what He told us to do when He told us to do it. Let us not forget how many times we sin when our thoughts or attitudes do not reflect His glory. However, God is always ready to forgive us. First John 1:9 states: *"If we confess our sins, he is faithful and just to forgive us our sins, and to cleanse us from all unrighteousness."* If we believe this, why have we not forgiven ourselves for something we have done in the past or are still doing?

I stated before that sometimes we feel like we have done some things so horrible that even God will not forgive us. We do not ask for His forgiveness because we have not forgiven ourselves. We feel that what we have done is too sick, shameful, and sinful. This unforgiveness of self leads to unending mental, physical, and spiritual torment. As a result, we often live under the heavy burden of guilt, low self-esteem, and a myriad of other issues.

Do we realize that when we do not forgive ourselves, we sin against God and put ourselves above Him? Jesus said that every kind of sin may be forgiven except blasphemy against the Holy Spirit (Matt. 12:31-32; Mark 3:28-29; Luke 12:10). If Jesus said that the Father would forgive us for *everything* except blasphemy (and we have not blasphemed against the Holy Spirit), then whatever we have done is forgivable!

Not only do we need to forgive others and sometimes ourselves, some of us feel we have been wronged by God, and we are harboring unforgiveness against Him.

FORGIVING GOD

"For I consider that the sufferings of this present time are not worth comparing with the glory that is to be revealed to us. For the creation waits with eager longing for the revealing of the sons of God." Romans 8:18-19, ESV

"As a number of us have already acknowledged, when we talk about our struggle to forgive God we don't really mean we think God has sinned against us. What we mean is that we feel that God has wronged us in ways that have broken our hearts, and allowed pain and loss into our lives that has frightened, confused, and disillusioned us."[3] (If we are angry with God, we must acknowledge to Him what He already knows.)

Some of us are honestly angry with God for the pain of our past or the predicament of our present. We do not like the families we were born into, our parents, our siblings, etc. We are angry with God for our loved ones being gone. We are angry with God because it seems the more we believe in Him, the less we receive from Him, and it seems like everyone else has received the desires of their heart, except us. We are angry with God because we have asked Him for some things that we have not gotten, and it seems that He is either not listening or really does not care.

Let us look at our friend Job. Job was a man who was called perfect and upright by God's own description (Job 1:1). God blessed him with a lovely family and a wealth of riches, cattle, and land. However, God allowed Satan to test Job. Satan was permitted to cause Job to be gravely ill and to take away everything Job had, but he was not allowed to touch Job's soul. Satan believed that once these deeds were done, Job would turn on God, His maker and provider. Some might say that Job had a right to be angry with God, for he had served God with all his heart, soul, and mind. When others turned their backs on God, Job followed God. Yet, he still lost everything. However, with all that Job lost and went through, He remained faithful to His Creator and His Lord. Make no mistake; Job did get a little weary when he cursed the day that he was born. He even questioned God regarding his suffering when his friends told him that it must have been something wrong that he did to cause his misfortune. However, when his wife confirmed her anger with God by telling

Job to curse God and die, Job said, *"All the days of my appointed time will I wait, till my change come"* (Job 14:14b).

Perhaps anger with God is why many of us do not regularly attend church, pray with fervency, or serve in our spiritual callings with as much zeal as we should. Is this because we feel God has let us down? We wonder if He has forgotten about us. God tells us in His word that we are not exempt from trials and tribulations (John 16:33). However, God has not forgotten about us! David said in Psalm 46:1 that God is *"a very present help in trouble"* (emphasis mine). God said, *"When thou passest through the waters, I will be with thee; and through the rivers, they shall not overflow thee: when thou walkest through the fire, thou shalt not be burned; neither shall the flame kindle upon thee"* (Isaiah 43:2).

*+

Forgiveness is one of the basic tenets of Christianity. When we do not forgive, we are destroying ourselves physically, mentally, and spiritually. We must practice forgiveness, even for our own health. Dr. Frederic Luskin, author of *Forgive for Good*, asserts, "People who forgive show less depression, anger, and stress and more hopefulness."[4] In relation to the physical health benefits, he notes that forgiving can also "help save on the wear and tear on our organs, reduce the wearing out of the immune system, and allow people to feel more vital."

> To forgive is to set a prisoner free and discover the prisoner was you!

In order to be forgiven by God, we must first learn to forgive others. In order to experience the true love and forgiveness of God for ourselves, we must draw nigh unto Him and learn of Him.

Then and only then can we truly know we are who He says we are!

Complete the workbook lesson on "Forgiveness."

14

I AM WHO GOD SAYS I AM

"And if children, then heirs; heirs of God, and joint-heirs with Christ;
if so be that we suffer with him, that we may be
also glorified together." Romans 8:17

Before we can know who we are as women, we must first know who we are in Christ. The truth of the matter is that apart from Christ, we are nothing! Revelation 4:11 says, *"Thou art worthy, O Lord, to receive glory and honour and power: for thou hast created all things, and for thy pleasure they are and were created"* (emphasis added). We must know we were made by God for His pleasure. We must give Him honor and glory simply because He is God: *"Before the mountains were brought forth, or ever thou hadst formed the earth and the world, even from everlasting to everlasting, thou art God"* (Psalm 90:2). We have been bought with a price.

In *The Purpose Driven Life*[1] by Rick Warren, there is a chapter titled "You are Not an Accident." Regardless of how you may have been conceived—even if it were through a violent act of rape or through incest—your focus must not be on how you were created but on why God allowed you to be born. We do not get to choose when we are conceived. We do not get to choose by whom we are conceived. We do not get to choose the color of our skin, the color of our eyes, or the texture of our hair. We do not get to choose the size of our lips, busts, or hips. We did not get to choose the day we were born. We did not have any say in these matters at all. Nevertheless, what we do have control over as a creation is getting to know our Creator and why He purposed us to live. What we do have control over, under normal circumstances, are things such as whom we have sex with. Is this the person you would choose to be the father of your child? If not, think twice. No protection or birth control is pregnancy proof. If this is not the person you would want to deal with as the father of your child for the rest of your life, it is best to abstain. Abortion is not an option!

Our search for why we are on planet earth is a search we all must pursue: it is our search for significance. We are not to be identified by the circumstances from whence we came but rather by the purpose for which we were born to fulfill. So often, we waste precious time trying to find our purpose in life and trying to find our identity when we come into the body of Christ. All we have to do is look in the Word of God.

This is not an attempt to teach a Bible study lesson. However, through my years of experience in women's ministry, one thing I have learned is that until people are confident in who they are and, more importantly, begin to develop a closer relationship with the One they claim they belong to, they will continue to lack some vital necessities needed to begin the healing process and live a victorious life. When we become confident in who we are and whose we are, we can hold on and be assured that we can move through this life facing whatever challenges come our way because of the promises God has made to us.

I designed the exercises in the corresponding workbook to help us stand taller in our faith, to enable us to hold our heads up, and to give us the artillery needed to combat the adversary's opinion of who we are. Many times, the adversary's opinion of who we are comes through those who allow themselves to be used by him and those who callously spout out their negative views of who we are. In doing so, they reveal their own issues and inward pain because hurting people usually hurt other people. Therefore, we must fight against these satanic tactics and not allow the adversary or anyone else to determine for us who we are and how we ought to feel about ourselves.

We must S.T.A.N.D.:

> **S**uit up for the battle
> **T**alk to God often
> **A**djust our attitude
> **N**ever allow anyone to define our self-worth
> **D**etermine only to believe we are who God says we are

We will go forward with the reassurance that we are somebody simply because we belong to the Master. We no longer want to be defined by our painful past, our excruciating experiences, or the never-ending negative views of others, for we are who God says we are. Who we are in Christ begins and ends with who God says we are, our relationship with Him, and our purpose in Him. For it was in His hands that we were shapened. It is in His hands that we find love, forgiveness, and peace, and now we can move from the horrendous hands that have hurt us to the holy hands that can heal us.

**Complete the workbook lesson on
"I Am Who God Says I Am."**

15

HANDS

"And he took the damsel by the hand, and said unto her, Talitha cumi; which is, being interpreted, Damsel, I say unto thee, arise."
Mark 5:41

"Though I walk in the midst of trouble, thou wilt revive me: thou shalt stretch forth thine hand against the wrath of mine enemies, and thy right hand shall save me. The Lord will perfect that which concerneth me." Psalm 138:7-8a

The lingering, horrifying memory of the touch from the sick, sinister, slimy hands that stole our innocence still haunt many of us today. Even with ministry and moving toward wholeness, memories still exist. If we could erase our memory, that would solve so many of our problems. If we could just replace the portion of our brains that housed those memories, we would, but the reality of the situation is that we know we cannot. So what do we do?

Through ministry, prayer, and Bible study—allowing God's Word and His promises to come alive in our lives—we can overcome anything. We cannot continue to reject others, especially males, because we fear being touched. We cannot continue to cheat ourselves and others of lavishing totally in the power of touch because of the hands that touched us so inappropriately.

It is the motive behind the touch that is crucially important.

The difference in how and why one is touched, I believe, lies in the heart. The power of human touch, with the right motive, can be one of the most rewarding experiences. Touch can be more satisfying than just a physical experience.

****

The word hand is found 500 times in the Bible, and hands is found 438. Why is this important? Isaiah 64:8 says, *"But now, O Lord, thou art our father; we are the clay, and thou our potter; and we all are the work of thy hand."* Genesis 2:7 reads: *"And the Lord God formed man of the dust of the ground, and breathed into his nostrils the breath of life; and man became a living soul."* Therefore, we can conclude that it was by the hands of God that man was formed. Up until this point, God had spoken everything else into existence.

Why did God make it a point to take His very hands to make us as opposed to speaking us into existence? He made us different because we were His special creation. We would be the only creation that would be in His image, after His likeness, trichotomous—body, mind and soul.

Genesis chapter 1 verses 26 and 27 state, *"And God said, Let us make man in our image, after our likeness . . . So God created man in his own image, in the image of God created he him; male and female created he them."* God formed us with His hands because He wanted to give us what He had not given any other creature, a part of Him, which required His personal touch. God took special care in how He created us. He touched us. From the beginning of our very existence, God touched us, His human creation.

The word touch is found 48 times in the Bible. The first

mention of the spoken word touch in the Bible ironically is recorded as spoken by the first woman in Genesis 3:3. Why is it significant that the woman first mentioned the word touch? Why did the word touch come from her lips and not the man's? Was it because of how she was created? As time went by, God saw that *"it [was] not good for the man to be alone"* (Genesis 2:18, NLT). He caused Adam to fall into a deep sleep and by His hands performed the first surgery without anesthesia. God took a rib from Adam's side, and with His hands, He fashioned woman. God had formed man from the dust (touch), but then He went *into* man, took a rib out of him (touch), and fashioned the rib into woman (touch). Would this be considered a touch, after a touch, after a touch?

Could this be why touch was important to the woman? Had the woman been touched in a way the male had not been touched? Adam was fashioned from the dust of the ground, and God blew the breath of life into him (first touch). Then God took man and placed him eastward in the garden (second touch). Although God created man first, the essence of woman was already there within the man. When God took the dust to form man, in a sense, woman was there within the substance of the dust. When God reached inside man and took his rib out, woman was inside the rib, as well. God took the rib and formed woman, giving her three touches by the hand of God. Many of us experienced the horror of physical hands that touched us in inappropriate ways. Hands of thieves who stole our sexual innocence. Hands that touched and violated our bodies. For me, it was in an actual closet that the hands grasped, groped, grabbed, poked, prodded, and preyed on me. Emotionally and spiritually, however, the touch of God restored me. God gave the little four-year-old girl a way of escape. He extended to the woman of 46 His hand, which she gripped with all that was within her, as He reminded her, *"I will restore to you the years that the locust hath eaten"* (Joel 2:25).

Being touched by the hands of God is like no other touch we will ever experience. Peter's mother-in-law can attest to the power of the touch of God's hand, *"But Simon's wife's mother lay sick with a fever, and they told Him about her at once. So He came and took her by the hand and lifted her up, and immediately the fever left her. And she served them"* (Mark 1:30-31, NKJV).

The woman with the issue of blood can testify about the power of touch. She was the one who dared to reach out to touch Jesus, for she proclaimed, *"If I may but touch his garment, I shall be whole"*(Matthew 9:21). Similarly, the woman who was trapped for 18 long years in her bent over body (her closet), and could in no wise lift up herself, is another witness to the power of touch. Jesus saw her, called her unto Him, took her by the hand, lifted her up, and immediately, she was made straight (Luke 13:10-13).

In the closet, the hands of hurt and evil were ever present but so were the hands of healing and eternal comfort. I now know that as God was with the three Hebrew boys in the fiery furnace, so was He there in the midst of my closet.

It was women's ministry that caused my blinded eyes to open and realize I had remained a prisoner in that damnable closet from the age of 4 until 46. It was in women's ministry where my life changed forever, physically, emotionally, and spiritually. Ministry has helped me realize that the power of freedom was within my reach. God showed me through ministry that the door had already been opened. Jesus was The Open Door that was waiting for me. Ministry showed me that if I reached out to take the hand that offered freedom and healing, that touch would make me whole. God, being omnipresent, had to present His hand from the outside, from the light, and reach inside to where I was trapped in darkness in order to escort me outside to the marvelous light. The Light (Jesus) reached into the closet to touch me and take me by the hand, away from the evil, sinister hands that violated me for so long.

Sin caused the power of touch to become evil because man took his hands and did many evil things with them. We may have been hurt at the hand of someone else, but the hand of Jesus can lift us from death to life. We may have been hurt at the hand of someone else, but the holy hands of God have made (or will make) us enjoy and appreciate the power of touch once again.

Women, if you have ever experienced the pain of being touched inappropriately by the hands of another person, do not allow that awful occurrence to rob you of the joy of experiencing a healthy touch and being able to reach out and touch others, as well. Perhaps this ran through the mind of the sculptor of the infamous Venus de Milo as he designed her with no arms for which to reach and no hands for which to touch.

Thanks be to God the hand of Jesus has already lifted many of us from death to life. And I encourage those who are reading this book who have not been lifted yet to hold on because help is on the way! God will turn your mourning into dancing!

God will touch us and make us whole. Songwriter William Gaither confirmed this when he penned these words in his famous hymn, "He touched me and made me whole."[1] The Lord is saying to each of us, "I say unto thee women, Talitha cumi, rise!"

While he yet spake, there came from the ruler of the synagogue's house certain which said, 'Thy daughter is dead: why troublest

thou the Master any further?' As soon as Jesus heard the word that was spoken, he saith unto the ruler of the synagogue, 'Be not afraid, only believe.' And he suffered no man to follow him, save Peter, and James, and John the brother of James. And he cometh to the house of the ruler of the synagogue, and seeth the tumult, and them that wept and wailed greatly. And when he was come in, he saith unto them, 'Why make ye this ado, and weep? the damsel is not dead, but sleepeth.' And they laughed him to scorn. But when he had put them all out, he taketh the father and the mother of the damsel, and them that were with him, and entereth in where the damsel was lying. And he took the damsel by the hand, and said unto her, 'Talitha cumi'; which is, being interpreted, 'Damsel, I say unto thee, arise.' And straightway the damsel arose, and walked; for she was of the age of twelve years. And they were astonished with a great astonishment.
(Mark 5:35-42)

AFTERWORD

Venus De Milo is a magnificent Roman statue. It is made of marble and represents Venus, the goddess of love. The Greeks call her Aphrodite. This statue is one of the great treasures of the Louvre museum in Paris. It is called the *Venus de Milo*, or *Venus Melos*, because it was found on the Greek island of Melos in 1820. For hundreds of years, the statue remained hidden in an underground cave near the ruins of an ancient theater. During these centuries, the statue suffered considerable damage. When it was found, the arms had been fragmented into so many pieces until the sculpture was impossible to repair. To many, she represents the perfect symbol of total acceptance, complete receptivity, especially to the man who loved her. One idea is that without arms, such a beautiful woman could never keep at a distance those who truly loved her.

How many men are looking for a Venus de Milo? A woman who does not possess arms to push him away? It is my belief that many women, because of past pain, keep men at a distance. How sad it is for a woman to deny herself of the most beautiful experiences that humans can have with humans, love without the demonic barrier of fear. How wondrous a gift our Creator has made available to humans—love without reservation. Such love is a soothing salve, a bountiful balm from beyond the blissful boundaries of lustful desire. Such love is a healing ointment, a treasure that keeps on refreshing its possessors with fountains of living water. Such love would transcend anything earthly. Such love would quench our deepest human thirst.

As I close this final chapter of what is really my life works, I remind you, especially women, that the human search for significance in life on earth is at its core the search of every human being for God's divine love in human form. It is the search for a love that is unfettered by fear, undiminished by distance, unmarred by malicious words, unseared by selfishness, unencumbered by caution, undaunted by debilitating doubt, undimmed by the accumulation of days, and unperturbed by the passage of time. As women, especially, we must never allow the fear of hurt to dissuade us from believing that this level of love exists. We must never cheapen ourselves by accepting tawdry gifts as a substitute for the only gift with real intrinsic value—true love. If necessary, we must spend the remainder of our days in its noble pursuit, illusive as it may sometimes appear. We must never settle for second best in the one shot at life on earth that our Creator has granted us.

The hands that sculptured the lovely Venus were obviously gentle hands and, almost certainly, loving hands. No one knows how or why the arms of such a lovely creature were broken off. Was the sculptor himself the culprit of the disfiguring deed? Could it have been he was in love with the voluptuous Venus only to have his love spurned? Or was she so afraid of being hurt by such a lover that she held him at arm's length? Or was it simply the callous handling of such a fine but fragile figure (just as many women today are mishandled) that caused her arms to just fall off? Certainly, we are left only to speculate what could have been, but women, do not allow your lives to be languished in the sad and frightening valley of *what could have been*. Let us confront our fears, submit to the Savior to bind our wounds, and revisit no more the tomb of past pain. Instead, "screw your courage to the sticking place"[1] and venture forth into the radiant sunlight of the promises of God. The Savior promised in what we call the beatitudes, *"Blessed are the pure in heart: for they shall see God"* (Matthew 5:8). It is my sincere belief that if women would look toward the horizon beyond the hurts they have experienced, on a clear day, beyond their tears, they will be able to see the Adams for which they were created.

Bone of his bone and flesh of his flesh, in all the glorious splendor of that first spring morning when the word "Woman" caused the birds to sing, the young lions to roar, the leopards to leap, the coyotes to howl, the crickets to chirp, and all of creation to gaze aghast in awe. There she stood, Woman, in all her wondrous splendor, reflecting the awesome and superb ability of the Creator. Woman, in all her dazzling beauty, possessor of a physical form that stood alone in the brilliant and spectacular sunlight of that new day. Yes, Woman, the crown jewel of creation, a fitting masterpiece that represented the Creator's final offering to the planet. I can but imagine Adam, awe-struck at her physical form, awe-struck and amazed at her marvelous copper-tone hue shimmering beneath the sun-lit sky. The moment was such that a hush was audible throughout heaven, after which the angelic host suddenly burst into an operatic crescendo of praise. It seemed that all of heaven spontaneously knew the world beneath would never be the same. The mere sound of the man's utterance of the word "Woman" resonated throughout the grassy garden region. The foliage seemed to sway slightly, in a balmy breeze, as Adam gazed at the most beautiful of all creatures, glistening in the dew and glistering in outward luster. Woman, the one whom Adam would later call Eve, was representative of the beauty that is within the grasp of any woman who yields to the Master's molding hand. In their first day together, the two surely became one (Genesis 2:24). That day can dawn in the life of every woman of virtue who has the will to wait and the determination to present herself before God just as she is and never again permit herself to descend into the valley of doubt but rather bask in the hope of heaven. Then, and only then, will we be ready to walk hand in hand with Adam through the garden of life. Then, and only then, will the arms of male and female extend themselves beyond fear and serve out their true purpose of embracing one another with all the passion that both hold captive within. It will be then that women will be where they were created to be—home with their Adam in Eden, with no serpent to beguile them ever again. Only then can women lie asleep peacefully, secure within the loving arms of their Adam, under the tree of life—arms enfolded within his, invisible to the human eye. Women, emerge from the dark and hideous closet of the past and enter into the garden of love that awaits your presence. Certainly, the voice of your Adam can be heard beckoning in the distance, *"Come. I have waited for what seemed like an eternity for you to come unto me."*

****

One balmy and sunny April morning in 2006, I was in route to work. Suddenly, I decided to stop by the grocery store to pick up a few items for lunch. I scurried about the nearly empty store from one aisle to the other. Having gathered my items, I took my place in the "10 items or less express line," as there were only two people ahead of me. As I stood there mentally rehearsing my agenda for work, I heard a deep, baritone voice from behind say, "Hello, Shirley." Somewhat startled, I turned around, and to my surprise, there stood the male relative who had sexually abused me in the dark closet nearly five decades earlier. We awkwardly went through the cool but cordial motions of embracing, but even then, the eerie and dark memories that haunted me within the shadows of that closet loomed ominously within my mind. As the thoughts raced back through nearly 50 years of pain, I spoke, and for a few moments, we exchanged small talk and niceties concerning the family. I attempted to look into his eyes, but the childhood shame seemed to lure my focus away. It was then that he spoke of the crime that had been committed against my virtue. He simply said, "I am sorry for what I did." Seven is the number of completion, and the seven words of his apology, that seemed so filled with remorse, were as a soothing salve to a heart that had suffered from nearly half a century of confusion, guilt, and anger. He did not have to clarify what he was sorry for because deep inside both of us knew all too well. It was then that I could look into his eyes. It was then that I came to the realization that through all of the years that had transpired since the violation of my innocence, he, too, was held captive within a hellish and horrible closet much worse than mine. At that moment, almost in an instance, all of the confusion was somehow alleviated. All of the guilt automatically vanquished, and I was acquitted of all of the anger I had harbored, as both of us, I believe, became free! As I accepted his apology, I finally became loosed from the fetters of frustration of my youthful, and most of my adult, years. As the cashier greeted me, I could return her greeting as a free woman. As I bade him a forgiving and almost affectionate adieu, I could all but feel the hand of God bringing about a new day of freedom and liberty in the both of us.

As I was walked through the automatic doors of that grocery store, it was if the Lord Himself had opened the doors to a new beginning, for I was leaving a world of pain and anguish once and for all, never again to return. Surely, we both were liberated from a past of darkness and despair. When the sunlight of that early spring morning met the ebony hue of my smiling face, I could all but hear the loving hands of a healing God applauding the redemption of two of His hurting children. As I drove to work, I reflected on the fact that I entered that grocery store to get a few items for lunch and exited it able to dine at the communion table as a whole woman. He died a year later, but I am convinced that he died free—as free as a soul redeemed by God could be. Thank God for the healing hands of a loving Savior, for He took us both by the hand and brought us out of the closet. As I arrived at work, I could all but hear in the distant breeze the words of one of my favorite songs that became my reality, *"I can't even walk unless He holds my hand."*

NOTES

Preface
[1] Dr. Maya Angelou was born in 1928 in St. Louis, Missouri. She is known as a renaissance woman with interests and achievements in dance, filmmaking, television, music, and most notably, poetry. Her autobiographical work *I Know Why the Caged Bird Sings* was published in 1970 and has received national and international acclaim.

Yvonne's Story
[1] According to Greek mythology, Pandora, the first woman on earth, was given many talents by the gods, including beauty, music, and persuasion. Eventually, to their detriment, they also gave her the gift of curiosity. After being given to Prometheus' brother (Prometheus' punishment for stealing fire from Zeus), Pandora was given a box with instructions not to open it. Compelled by her curiosity, she opened the box anyway and released evil into the world.

The Invisible Child
[1] A pseudonym is used for anonymity.

Dead Woman Walking
[1] This letter is reprinted with permission. It first appeared online at www.raiin.org.
[2] "Statistics," Rape, Abuse and Incest National Network, accessed September 27, 2011, http://www.rainn.org/statistics.

Coming out of the Closet
[1] The full verse to the "Humpty Dumpty" nursery rhyme is: Humpty Dumpty sat on a wall / Humpty Dumpty had a great fall / All the King's horses, and all the King's men / Couldn't put Humpty together again!

² T.D. Jakes, *Woman Thou Art Loosed* (Shippensburg, PA: Destiny Image, 2006).

The Need for Ministry

¹ A study of African American churches found that women comprised the majority of the congregations, but pastors were predominately male. Linda Lowen, "The Role of African American Women in the Black Church: Women Outnumber Men in the Pews, Yet are Rarely Seen in the Pulpit," Women's Issues, accessed September 27, 2011, http://womensissues.about.com/od/communityconnection/a/blackwomenchurc.htm.

² "What are the Major Challenges that U.S. Congregations Face?" U.S. Congregations, accessed September 27, 2011, http://www.uscongregations.org/challenges.htm.

Who Am I?

¹ Cynthia Hicks and Robert Hicks, *The Feminine Journey: Understanding the Biblical Stages of a Woman's Life* (Colorado: NavPress, 1994).

² Emily A. Impett and Letitia Anne Peplau, "'His' and 'Her' Relationships? A Review of the Empirical Evidence." In *The Cambridge Handbook of Personal Relationships,* ed. Anita L. Vangelisti and Daniel Perlman (New York: Cambridge University Press, 2006), 276.

³ Robin L. Smith, *Lies at the Altar: the Truth about Great Marriages* (New York: Hyperion, 2006).

⁴ Camille Noe Pagan, "Depression Hurts," ForbesWoman, http://www.forbes.com/2009/07/07/depression-antidepressants-psychotherapy-forbes-woman-health-stress.html.

⁵ Myrna M. Weissman and Mark Olfson, "Depression in Women: Implications for Health Care Research," *Science* 269 (1995): 799, http://www.sciencemag.org/content/269/5225/799.full.pdf.

⁶ "Depression in Women: Understanding the Gender Gap," Mayo Clinic, http://www.mayoclinic.com/health/depression/MH00035.

⁷ Ibid.

[8] In Psalms, Selah represents pause, to rest.

He Came to Set the Captives Free

[1] Elvina Hall, "Jesus Paid it All,"
http://www.cyberhymnal.org/htm/j/p/jpaidall.htm.
[2] J.W. Van Deventer, "I Surrender All,"
http://www.cyberhymnal.org/htm/i/s/isurrend.htm.

Life is Less than Perfect

[1] Ruth Haley Barton, *Becoming a Woman of Strength: 14 Life Challenges for Women* (Colorado Springs: Shaw Books, 2000).
[2] Viktor E. Frankl, *Man's Search for Meaning* (Massachusetts: Beacon Press, 2006), 103-04.
[3] "Edwin Markham Quotes,"
http://thinkexist.com/quotation/for_all_your_days_prepare-and_meet_them_ever/252461.html.

Issues, Issues, Issues

[1] When the dilation and curettage (D&C) procedure is performed, the cervix is dilated (opened up), and suction is used to remove uterine contents. Sometimes, the uterine wall is scraped using a curette instrument to ensure all contents are removed.
[2] Otherwise known as "saline amniocentesis," "salting out," or a "hypertonic saline abortion," this procedure is usually performed after 16 weeks of pregnancy. A concentrated salt solution is injected into the amniotic fluid, which kills the baby by acute salt poisoning.
[3] Partial birth abortion is a pregnancy termination method that is performed in the mid to late second trimester. This method results in the death and intact removal of a fetus from the uterus (by delivery of the fetus feet first, followed by the puncturing and suctioning of its skull). This procedure became illegal in the United States in 2008.
[4] RU486 is also known as the "Early Option" pill. It is a chemical

compound that can induce abortion in women up to nine weeks pregnant. RU486 is an artificial steroid that interferes with progesterone, a hormone that stimulates the uterine lining nourishing a developing child. When the RU 486 pill is taken, the unborn child is deprived of essential nutrients and starves to death. Then, the baby and decomposed uterine lining are removed from the body.

5 "Prohibiting Dangerous Abortive Drugs Like RU-486 and ellaOne," National Pro-Life Alliance, http://www.prolifealliance.com/ru-486%20ban.htm.

6 "RU486 – The Pill, The Process, The Problems," California ProLife Council, http://www.californiaprolife.org/resources/abortion_information/ru486/.

7 "Bans on 'Partial-Birth' Abortion," Guttmacher Institute, *State Policies in Brief,* http://www.guttmacher.org/statecenter/spibs/spib_BPBA.pdf.

8 Sandra G. Boodman, special writer for *The Washington Post,* reported that there were 1.2 million abortions performed in 2005. In the same year, there were 341,000 appendectomies, 398,000 gallbladder removals and 575,000 hysterectomies, http://www.washingtonpost.com/wp-dyn/content/article/2009/08/28/AR2009082802785.html.

9 Kathleen, *Healing from Sexual Abuse* (Illinois: InterVarsity Press, 1991).

10 Kathleen, *Healing from Sexual Abuse,* 6.

11 Donna St. George, "Murder in the Making," *The Washington Post,* August 27, 2000, http://www.highbeam.com/doc/1P2-539744.html.

12 Linda M. Woolf, "Spousal Abuse: a Global Problem," Women and Global Human Rights," http://www.webster.edu/~woolflm/domesticviolence.html.

13 Gautama Siddharta, http://thinkexist.com/quotation/holding_on_to_anger_is_like_grasp inga_hot_coal/12958.html .

14 Gary J. Oliver and H. Normal Wright, *Good Women Get Angry: a Woman's Guide to Handling Anger, Depression, Anxiety and Stress* (Michigan: Vine, 1995), 90.

[15] Julie Baumgardner, "The United States' $100 billion Man," First Things First, http://firstthings.org/page/media/the-family-column/the-united-states-100-billion-man.

[16] T.J. Matthews, Sally C. Curtin, and Marian F. MacDorman, "Infant Mortality Statistics from the 1998 Period Linked Birth/Infant Death Data Set," *National Vital Statistics Reports* (Maryland: National Center for Health Statistics, 2000).

[17] Jay D. Teachman, "The Childhood Living Arrangements of Children and the Characteristics of Their Marriages," *Journal of Family Issues* 25 (2004).

[18] Tracy L. Snell and Danielle C. Morton, "Women in Prison: Survey of Prison Inmates," *Bureau of Justice Statistics Special Report* (Washington, DC: US Department of Justice, 1991).

[19] Andrea J. Sedlak and Diane D. Broadhurst, "The Third National Incidence Study of Child Abuse and Neglect: Final Report," *U.S. Department of Health and Human Services* (Washington, DC: National Center on Child Abuse and Neglect, 1996).

Taking out the Trash

[1] Charles Albert Tindley was born the son of a slave in 1851. It is said that a friend visited Tindley, and after listening to that friend's worries, Tindley responded, "My advice to you is put all your troubles in a sack, take 'em to the Lord, and leave 'em there." NetHymnal, accessed October 7, 2011, http://www.cyberhymnal.org/htm/l/e/leaveitt.htm.

[2] Erykah Badu, "Bag Lady," *Mama's Gun*, 2000.

[3] "William Newton Clarke Quotes," http://thinkexist.com/quotes/william_newton_clarke/.

Forgiveness

[1] Nancy Leigh DeMoss, *Choosing Forgiveness: Your Journey to Freedom* (Illinois: Moody, 2006), 25.

2 Stormie Omartian, *The Power of a Praying Woman Deluxe Edition* (Oregon: Harvest House, 2002), 47.
3 Mart de Haan and Friends, "Been Thinking About: Forgiving God," RBC Ministries, accessed March 30, 2008, http://old.beenthinking.org/2008/04/01/one-mans-anger/.
4 Fred Luskin, *Forgive for Good* (New York: HarperCollins, 2002), xv; 88.

I Am Who God Says I Am

1 Rick Warren, *The Purpose Driven Life* (Michigan: Zondervan, 2004).

Hands

1 William J. Gaither wrote the words and provided the score to the hymn "He Touched Me" in 1963.

Afterword

1 William Shakespeare, "MacBeth," Bartleby.com, http://www.bartleby.com/46/4/17.html